Social security:
A new consensus

INTERNATIONAL LABOUR OFFICE • GENEVA

Contents

Preface v

Resolution and Conclusions concerning social security,
International Labour Conference, 89th Session, 2001 1

RESOLUTION CONCERNING SOCIAL SECURITY 1
CONCLUSIONS CONCERNING SOCIAL SECURITY 1

Report of the Committee on Social Security,
International Labour Conference, 89th Session, 2001 (extracts) 7

INTRODUCTION 7
Point 1. Social security and economic development 11
Point 2. Extension of social security coverage 13
Point 3. Income security for the unemployed and employment 15
Point 4. Equality between men and women 18
Point 5. Financing of social security and ageing 23
Point 6. Social dialogue and ILO activities 25
Appendix 29

Social security: Issues, challenges and prospects
Report VI to the International Labour Conference, 89th Session, 2001 31

INTRODUCTION 31

CHAPTER I. *The prospects for social security* 33
    The global context 34
    Social security and decent work 38
    Some key issues 40
        Social security, employment and development 40
        Extending the personal coverage of social protection 40
        Contributing to gender equality 40
        Sustainable financing for social protection 41
        Expanding social dialogue 41
    The aim of the report 41

CHAPTER II. *Social security, employment and development* 42
    The social and economic impact of social security 42
        Social security expenditure, unemployment and growth 43
        Productivity and social stability 45
        Employer contributions and international competitiveness 47
        Unemployment benefits, unemployment and employment 49
        Early retirement 49
    Unemployment benefits and employment promotion 50
        Relevant international labour standards 50
        Industrialized countries 51
        Middle-income developing countries 52

Other developing countries 53
Conclusion: Linking social security with employment
and development policies 54

CHAPTER III. *Extending the personal coverage of social protection* 56
The right to social security 56
The problem of non-coverage 57
Policies to achieve the extension of coverage 59
    The economic, social and political context 59
    Strategies for extending social protection 60
Conclusions 67

CHAPTER IV. *Gender equality* 69
International labour standards and gender equality 70
The link between social protection and gender 71
The impact of labour market inequalities on different forms of
social protection 71
Measures to grant equality of treatment in social protection and
to promote gender equality through social protection 73
    Survivors' pensions 73
    Divorce and pension splitting 75
    Pensionable age 75
    Pension credits for persons with caring responsibilities 77
    Sex-differentiated annuity rates 77
    Parental leave and benefits and childcare services 78
    Child benefit 78
Conclusions 79

CHAPTER V. *The financing of social security* 80
Global trends in social security expenditure 80
Social security and its main challenges 82
    Does social security face an ageing crisis? 83
    Or does social security face a globalization crisis? 83
    Has social security reached the limits of its affordability? 84
National financing options 85
    Financing systems 86
    The indispensable role of government as ultimate financial guarantor 91
Globalization and social security financing 92
Conclusions 93

CHAPTER VI. *Strengthening and expanding social dialogue* 94
Actors in social protection 94
    Family and local solidarity networks 94
    Institutions of civil society 95
    Enterprises and the commercial market 95
    Government and social security institutions 96
    The international community 97
Partnerships for social protection 97
    Enhancing the effectiveness of social security 97
    Towards social protection for all 100
Conclusions 103

CHAPTER VII. *Implications for future ILO work* 104
Research and policy development 104
Providing a normative framework through standard setting 106
Technical cooperation and other means of action 108

SUGGESTED POINTS FOR DISCUSSION 110

STATISTICAL ANNEX 111

Preface

At its 89th Session in June 2001 the International Labour Conference held, as one of the main items on its agenda, a general discussion on social security. The Committee on Social Security attracted a high level of interest among delegates, with as many as 111 Government members, 59 Employer members and 79 Worker members,[1] and also numerous advisers and observers. No doubt this reflected the fact that the Committee had before it a number of highly controversial and potentially divisive issues. As in other Committees, special efforts were made to prepare the discussions carefully through wide consultation prior to the Conference. This paid off handsomely, as there was close cooperation, both in the Committee and in the group responsible for preparing the draft conclusions, between the social partners and key governmental spokespersons. As a result, the Committee was able to reach rapid agreement on a set of conclusions which reflects a consensus on many of the key issues and priorities. In particular, it was agreed that:

● highest priority should go to policies and initiatives to extend social security to those who have none;

● not only is security very important for the well-being of workers, their families and the community as a whole, but — if properly managed — it also enhances productivity and supports economic development;

● the ageing of the population affects both funded and pay-as-you-go pension systems: solutions are to be sought above all through measures to increase employment rates;

● the social partners have a strong role to play in the management of social security.

The Committee expressed very high expectations for future ILO action on social security. It did not make any recommendation about future standards-related activities, but stated that ILO activities on social security should be based on the relevant ILO social security standards,[2] the decent work goal and the Declaration of Philadelphia. It recommended a number of areas on which future ILO research and technical cooperation should focus. And it called for a major campaign on the extension of social security and for the ILO to urge governments to give higher priority to social security.

---

[1] Votes are weighted in order to achieve equality of voting strength between the three groups.

This volume contains the Committee's conclusions, large extracts from the report of the Committee's discussions, and the whole of the report which was prepared as a basis for the Committee's discussions.

The ILO does not usually single out the work of individual ILO staff members on reports of this nature. But I think it appropriate, on this occasion, to acknowledge the important contribution to this work made by Roger Beattie, who tragically died suddenly on 24 August.

I believe that the outcome of this discussion is a major step forward towards an ILO vision of social security which is in accordance with the needs of our times. Security is an essential element of the decent work agenda, social security a major instrument to achieve it. We must continue to build our capabilities, with universality our aim, and can do this now on the foundations of a very successful tripartite consensus.

Juan Somavia
Director-General

August 2001

---

² In the discussion, particular mention was made of the following Conventions, all of which have been categorized as up to date by the ILO Governing Body: the Social Security (Minimum Standards) Convention, 1952 (No. 102); the Equality of Treatment (Social Security) Convention, 1962 (No. 118); the Employment Injury Benefits Convention, 1964 [Schedule I amended in 1980] (No. 121); the Invalidity, Old-Age and Survivors' Benefits Convention, 1967 (No. 128); the Medical Care and Sickness Benefits Convention, 1969 (No. 130); the Maintenance of Social Security Rights Convention, 1982 (No. 157); the Employment Promotion and Protection against Unemployment Convention, 1988 (No. 168); and the Maternity Protection Convention, 2000 (No. 183).

Resolution and Conclusions concerning social security, International Labour Conference, 89th Session, 2001

Resolution concerning social security

The General Conference of the International Labour Organization, meeting in its 89th Session, 2001,

Having undertaken a general discussion on the basis of Report VI, *Social security: Issues, challenges and prospects*;

1. Adopts the following conclusions;

2. Invites the Governing Body of the International Labour Office:

(a) to give due consideration to them in planning future action on social security;

(b) to request the Director-General to take them into account both when preparing the programme and budget for the 2004-05 biennium and in allocating such resources as may be available during the 2002-03 biennium.

Conclusions concerning social security

1. In 1944 the Conference recognized "the solemn obligation of the International Labour Organization to further among the nations of the world programmes which will achieve … the extension of social security measures to provide a basic income to all in need of such protection and comprehensive medical care". It is time for a renewed campaign by the ILO to improve and extend social security coverage to all those in need of such protection. The Director-General is invited to address the conclusions set out below with the seriousness and urgency they deserve in order to overcome a fundamental social injustice affecting hundreds of millions in member States.

2. Social security is very important for the well-being of workers, their families and the entire community. It is a basic human right and a fundamental means for creating social cohesion, thereby helping to ensure social peace and social inclusion. It is an indispensable part of government social policy and an important tool to prevent and alleviate poverty. It can, through national solidarity and fair burden sharing,

contribute to human dignity, equity and social justice. It is also important for political inclusion, empowerment and the development of democracy.

3. Social security, if properly managed, enhances productivity by providing health care, income security and social services. In conjunction with a growing economy and active labour market policies, it is an instrument for sustainable social and economic development. It facilitates structural and technological changes which require an adaptable and mobile labour force. It is noted that while social security is a cost for enterprises, it is also an investment in, or support for, people. With globalization and structural adjustment policies, social security becomes more necessary than ever.

4. There is no single right model of social security. It grows and evolves over time. There are schemes of social assistance, universal schemes, social insurance and public or private provisions. Each society must determine how best to ensure income security and access to health care. These choices will reflect their social and cultural values, their history, their institutions and their level of economic development. The State has a priority role in the facilitation, promotion and extension of coverage of social security. All systems should conform to certain basic principles. In particular, benefits should be secure and non-discriminatory; schemes should be managed in a sound and transparent manner, with administrative costs as low as practicable and a strong role for the social partners. Public confidence in social security systems is a key factor for their success. For confidence to exist, good governance is essential.

5. Of highest priority are policies and initiatives which can bring social security to those who are not covered by existing systems. In many countries these include employees in small workplaces, the self-employed, migrant workers, and people — many of them women — active in the informal economy. When coverage cannot be immediately provided to these groups, insurance — where appropriate on a voluntary basis — or other measures such as social assistance could be introduced and extended and integrated into the social security system at a later stage when the value of the benefits has been demonstrated and it is economically sustainable to do so. Certain groups have different needs and some have very low contributory capacity. The successful extension of social security requires that these differences be taken into account. The potential of microinsurance should also be rigorously explored: even if it cannot be the basis of a comprehensive social security system, it could be a useful first step, particularly in responding to people's urgent need for improved access to health care. Policies and initiatives on the extension of coverage should be taken within the context of an integrated national social security strategy.

6. The fundamental challenge posed by the informal economy is how to integrate it into the formal economy. This is a matter of equity and social solidarity. Policies must encourage movement away from the informal economy. Support for vulnerable groups in the informal economy should be financed by society as a whole.

7. For persons of working age, the best way to provide a secure income is through decent work. The provision of cash benefits to the unemployed should there-

fore be closely coordinated with training and retraining and other assistance they may require in order to find employment. With the growth of economies in the future, education and skills of the workforce will be increasingly important. Education should be made available to all children to achieve adequate life skills, literacy and numeracy, and to facilitate personal growth and entry into the workforce. Lifelong learning is vital to maintain employability in today's economy. Unemployment benefits should be designed so that they do not create dependency or barriers to employment. Measures to make work financially more attractive than being in receipt of social security have been found effective. However benefits must be adequate. Where it is not deemed feasible to establish a system of unemployment benefits, efforts should be made to provide employment in labour-intensive public works and other projects, as is successfully done in a number of developing countries.

8. Social security should promote and be based on the principle of gender equality. However, this implies not only equal treatment for men and women in the same or similar situations, but also measures to ensure equitable outcomes for women. Society derives great benefit from the unpaid care which women in particular provide to children, parents and infirm family members. Women should not be systemically disadvantaged later in life because they made this contribution during their working years.

9. As a result of the vastly increased participation of women in the labour force and the changing roles of men and women, social security systems originally based on the male breadwinner model correspond less and less to the needs of many societies. Social security and social services should be designed on the basis of equality of men and women. Measures which facilitate the access of women to employment will support the trend towards granting women social security benefits in their own right, rather than as dependants. The nature of survivors' benefits needs to be kept under review and, in the event of reform, appropriate transitional provisions must be made to protect women whose life course and expectations have been based on the patterns of the past.

10. In most societies, continued inequalities in earnings between men and women tend to affect women's social security entitlements. This underlines the need for continued efforts to combat wage discrimination and to consider the desirability of introducing a minimum wage, where it does not already exist. Where either parent provides care for children, social security benefits for childcare purposes should be made available to the caregiver. Furthermore, each society should consider introducing positive discrimination in favour of women where systemic discrimination is faced.

11. The ageing of the population in many societies is a phenomenon which is having a significant effect on both advance-funded and pay-as-you-go pension systems and on the cost of health care. This is transparent in pay-as-you-go systems where a direct transfer takes place from contributors to pensioners. It is, however, just as real in advance-funded systems, where financial assets are sold to pay for pensions and purchased by the working generation. Solutions must be sought above all through measures to increase employment rates, notably of women, older workers, youth and persons with disabilities. Ways must also be found to achieve higher

levels of sustainable economic growth leading to additional numbers in productive employment.

12. In many developing countries, particularly in sub-Saharan Africa, the HIV/AIDS pandemic is having a catastrophic effect on every aspect of society. Its impact on the financial base of their social security systems is particularly acute, as the victims are concentrated among the working age population. This crisis calls for a much more urgent response through research and technical assistance by the ILO.

13. In pay-as-you-go defined benefit pension systems, risk is borne collectively. In systems of individual savings accounts, on the other hand, risk is borne by the individual. While this is an option which exists, it should not weaken solidarity systems which spread risks throughout the whole of the scheme membership. Statutory pension schemes must guarantee adequate benefit levels and ensure national solidarity. Supplementary and other negotiated pension schemes tailored more to the circumstances and contributory capacity of different groups in the labour force can be a valued addition to, but in most cases not a substitute for, statutory pension schemes. The social partners have an important role to play with regard to supplementary and other negotiated schemes, while the State's role is to provide an effective regulatory framework, and supervisory and enforcement mechanisms. Governments should consider that any support or tax incentives for these schemes should be targeted towards low- or medium-income earners. It is for each society to determine the appropriate mix of schemes, taking account of the conclusions of this general discussion and relevant ILO social security standards.

14. To be sustainable, the financial viability of pension systems must be guaranteed over the long term. It is therefore necessary to conduct regular actuarial projections and to implement the necessary adjustments sooner rather than later. It is essential to make a full actuarial evaluation of any proposed reform before adopting new legislation. There is a need for social dialogue on the assumptions to be used in the evaluation and on the development of policy options to address any financial imbalance.

15. Social security covers health care and family benefits and provides income security in the event of such contingencies as sickness, unemployment, old age, invalidity, employment injury, maternity or loss of a breadwinner. It is not always necessary, nor even in some cases feasible, to have the same range of social security provisions for all categories of people. However, social security systems evolve over time and can become more comprehensive in regard to categories of people and range of provisions as national circumstances permit. Where there is limited capacity to finance social security, either from general tax revenues or contributions — and particularly where there is no employer to pay a share of the contribution — priority should be given in the first instance to needs which are most pressing in the view of the groups concerned.

16. Within the framework of the basic principles set out earlier, each country should determine a national strategy for working towards social security for all. This should be closely linked to its employment strategy and to its other social policies. Tar-

geted social assistance programmes could be one means to commence the introduction of social security for excluded groups. As government resources are limited in developing countries, there may be a need to broaden the sources of funding for social security through, for example, tripartite financing. Where possible, government support might cover initial start-up costs, in-kind support in the form of facilities and equipment, or support for low-income groups. In order to be effective, initiatives to establish or extend social security require social dialogue. Any changes to established social security systems should be introduced with adequate protection for existing beneficiaries. Innovative pilot schemes are to be encouraged. Well-designed and cost-effective research is necessary in order to provide objective evaluations of pilot schemes. Research and technical assistance are necessary to improve governance of systems.

17. ILO activities in social security should be anchored in the Declaration of Philadelphia, the decent work concept and relevant ILO social security standards. Social security is not available to the majority of the world's people. This is a major challenge which needs to be addressed in the coming years. In that regard the Conference proposes that:

– a major campaign should be launched in order to promote the extension of coverage of social security;

– the ILO should call on governments to give the issue of social security a higher priority and offer technical assistance in appropriate cases;

– the ILO should advise governments and the social partners on the formulation of a national social security strategy and ways to implement it;

– the ILO should collect and disseminate examples of best practice.

Constituents should be encouraged to approach the ILO for special assistance to achieve outcomes which significantly improve the application of social security coverage to groups which are currently excluded. The programme is to be undertaken as soon as practicable and be subject to regular reports to the Governing Body.

18. The main areas identified for future social security research and meetings of experts are:

– the extension of coverage of social security;

– HIV/AIDS and its impact on social security;

– governance and administration of social security systems;

– equality, with an emphasis on gender and disability;

– ageing and its impact on social security;

– financing of social security;

– sharing of good practice.

These activities should form the basis for the further development of the ILO policy framework on social security and should be clearly linked to the further work programme, technical assistance priorities and activities of the ILO in this area.

19. The ILO's technical cooperation with governments and the social partners should include a wide range of measures, in particular:

– extending and improving social security coverage;

– developing innovative approaches in the area of social security to help people to move from the informal economy to the formal economy;

– improving the governance, financing and administration of social security schemes;

– supporting and training the social partners to participate in policy development and to serve effectively on joint or tripartite governing bodies of social security institutions;

– improving and adapting social security systems in response to changing social, demographic and economic conditions;

– introducing means to overcome discrimination in outcomes in social security.

20. The ILO should complete the programme of work as recommended above and must report regularly to the Governing Body on the results of that work, thereby enabling the Governing Body to monitor progress and decide how to proceed further.

21. The ILO should continue to develop interagency cooperation in the social security field, including with the International Social Security Association. The ILO should invite the IMF and the World Bank to support the conclusions adopted by the Conference and to join with the ILO in promoting social justice and social solidarity through the extension of comprehensive social security.

Report of the Committee on Social Security, International Labour Conference, 89th Session, 2001 (extracts)

Introduction

In her opening statement, the Chairperson thanked the Committee for the confidence it had placed in her. The objective of the general discussion was to establish an ILO vision of social security that, while continuing to be rooted in the basic principles of the ILO, responded to the new issues and challenges facing social security at a time of rapid economic, social and demographic change. The Committee had a unique opportunity to demonstrate to the world the continuing relevance of the ILO's mandate to ensure income security and health protection to all. The challenge before the Committee was to define a vision of social security which would guide the work of the Organization in the years to come.

The representative of the Secretary-General introduced the Office report. He emphasized the importance of the topic and pointed out the new economic and social context which had emerged since the main ILO instruments concerning social security had been adopted. Enormous changes had occurred at the social, economic, technological and political levels, bringing about new forms of employment, increased insecurity in a global economy, a growing informal sector, the transition of many countries to a market economy, and changes in gender relations and in family structures. There was a strong need to take stock of the existing situation. The Governing Body had thus decided that it would be best to tackle the problem initially through a general discussion that might subsequently lead to a standard-setting exercise. The report that had been prepared by the Office as a basis for the discussion examined five issues: social security, employment and development; the extension of social security coverage; gender equality; the financing of social security; and social dialogue. Various social and economic effects of social security protection were examined as well as possible ways of integrating social policies with employment promotion policies. Experience had shown that an effective social security system was a powerful tool for development and for the prevention or reduction of poverty. It contributed to social cohesion and stability and was a mainstay of a smooth-functioning, well-developed market economy. The problems faced in industrialized countries were clearly not the same as those faced in developing countries. Thus one of the major challenges before the Committee would be to transcend the limits of national debates and to adopt a truly international perspective relevant to all member States. The speaker stressed that social security reform was an area that benefited greatly from a tripartite approach. The Committee had a unique opportunity to produce an ambitious consensus, which could trace the broad outlines of social security for the coming years. It could breathe new life into the aspiration sweeping across all societies to provide social security to all, to reaffirm people's right to this protection, and to determine the ways and means to make this goal a reality. These deliberations would place the ILO at the centre of international debate on social security and orient its future work in this domain.

In order to facilitate the discussion, the representative of the Secretary-General proposed a reorganization into six themes of the suggested points for discussion appended to Report VI. This proposal was set out in document C.S.S./D.1. annexed (see p. 29) to this report.

The Worker Vice-Chairperson congratulated the Office on its fine report. The discussion of social security at the first International Labour Conference of the twenty-first century was timely and reflected the ILO's historical vision of justice and basic security for all. The 1944 Declaration of Philadelphia had set out a solemn obligation for the ILO to extend social security to all in need of protection, yet too little progress had been made in the intervening years. The present Conference setting was far removed from the reality of poverty where millions had no secure employment, health care or old-age benefits. New policies were needed to generate productive employment and greater personal opportunity, since these were the key to poverty reduction and to economic and social inclusion. The speaker called for constructive dialogue to meet the Committee's objectives: to define the issues, overcome the challenges and set out an ambitious but achievable vision for the new century. The ILO's place as an important institution in the achievement of decent standards of social security must be reaffirmed.

The Workers' group believed that social security involved equal rights and entitlements for men and women to adequate economic and social protection during unemployment, ill health, maternity, child rearing, loss of a breadwinner, disability and old age. Up to the present, the issue of family responsibilities had not yet been covered in a social security Convention. Gender equality in social security was a serious issue. Many social security systems produced much less favourable outcomes for women than for men. Among the factors contributing to unequal outcomes were women's lower average incomes, their predominance in sectors not covered by social security, interruptions in their working lives due to childbirth and family responsibilities, and qualifying conditions which restricted their access to benefits. Women and men should receive equal benefits. The factors leading to discrimination had to be addressed.

While globalization had the potential to improve living standards, it would not achieve this outcome through market forces alone. The provision of adequate social security benefits was necessary, alongside democratic government and sound economic management. Together they would make for a more productive and stable workforce and enhance the productivity of enterprises and economies. Recent social and economic changes had spurred the growth of a marginalized workforce. In developed countries, there was reduced job security, more part-time and casual workers, and more jobs in small and medium-sized enterprises. In developing countries, there was high unemployment and many informal workers engaged in unregulated, low-income, insecure work. Over time these informal workers must be assisted to move to freely chosen secure employment in the formal workforce. Structures which reinforced the existence of informal work should not be accepted. There was no ideal model for meeting the social security needs of marginalized groups. The Workers' group would support any initiatives that resulted in better social security outcomes for the excluded majority, but would not support approaches which called on the poor to provide for their own social security from their own limited resources. Further research and analysis of group-based social protection and microinsurance schemes by the ILO was needed, although the speaker expressed doubts regarding the capacity of such schemes to address needs adequately due to their limited coverage and financial means.

Regarding unemployment, the Workers' group believed that the provision of a secure job, lifelong training and/or retraining, and employment subsidies, where necessary, was the assistance most needed. Special attention to the needs of the long-term unemployed, youth and older workers was required. The ageing population had implications for social security systems, in light of the changing ratio of workers to the economically inactive, the need for additional health care, and expenditures on retirement pensions. There did not necessarily need to be radical changes to the retirement age or to benefit levels, however. Economic and social policy measures, appropriate labour market responses and improved productivity could all contribute to meeting the challenge of an ageing population. Better training and retraining of older workers, increased labour market participation of women, flexible or phased-in retirement schemes, adaptation of working hours and family-friendly workplace schemes were all options to be explored. The speaker stressed that existing benefit standards should be retained and pension entitlements safeguarded. The Workers' group believed that the following five principles should govern social security systems: the management of the system should provide a strong role for the social partners; the security of the system should be paramount; the schemes should be managed in a sound and transparent manner with regular reports to contributors and low administration costs; the State should ensure the sound operation of the system in the best interests of contributors; and there should be no direct or indirect discrimination. Workers did not believe that privatization offered an improved way of financing and administering social security. Indeed, experience had shown that high administrative costs had resulted in severely limited benefits. Governments' role as financial guarantors and underwriters of social security schemes was stressed, as was the importance of eradicating corruption, respecting core labour standards, and promoting the conditions for investment and growth. Workers were confident that reforms based on tripartite discussions would lead to greater security and would pay back significant dividends to communities. For their part, the Workers' group would engage constructively with the Employers' group and Government members to find practical solutions to difficult problems so that the light of social security would continue to burn brightly.

In his opening statement, the Employer Vice-Chairperson commended the Office for the research that had gone into the report, which would provide an excellent basis for discussion. He stressed the need for a flexible approach to extending social security to new groups and reforming existing schemes. He emphasized that no single model or solution could be replicated in all countries. Rather, social security had to be structured to take specific national conditions into account. These included not only economic development but also social and cultural norms. Around the world, many social security schemes were facing financial difficulties; and efforts to create new schemes where none existed were proving to be very difficult. These problems called for flexibility on the part of the Committee in looking for new directions and solutions.

Economic development and job creation were the surest forms of social security for workers. Adequate benefits could not be financed in the absence of these prerequisites. Given employers' central role in job creation, there was a need to avoid imposing an excessive burden on them for financing social security, as well as to target benefits effectively so as to keep costs affordable. In addition, there was a need for research by the ILO in several areas. These related to the relationship between social security and job creation and to finding new approaches to extend social security to the informal sector without overburdening the formal sector. All recent innovations had to be researched carefully, including those that involved privatization, and best practices had to be identified. Furthermore, the social partners needed to coordinate their policies on social security, since together they could help build the political will that made improvements in social security possible. The Employer Vice-Chairperson concluded that, beyond these general observations, the Employers' group would not elaborate further but would wait to hear additional Committee discussion. The representative of the Council of Europe stated that social security should be viewed as a fundamental human right. From this perspective, the establishment of national social security schemes was a landmark achievement of the twentieth century. The Council attached great importance to two legal instruments in the field of social security, the European Social Charter and the European Code of Social Security. Both provided basic principles which guided countries in building social security systems, and both were increasingly successful in terms of ratifications and the interest shown by Member States. These instruments gave the State overall responsibility for provision of social security, but States were challenged to consider new ways of exercising this authority in the twenty-first century. Social security policy could not stand alone but was inextricably linked with a country's legal framework and economic policies. Globalization had created problems which social security was useful in addressing, but it also required that social security itself be restructured to address the new challenges. The representative of the European Commission stated that there was a need to both modernize and improve social security systems and he described several recent actions by the Commission that placed greater emphasis on social security in its policy deliberations. These included the establishment of a Social Protection Committee and a decision to use the Open Method of Coordination in dealing with social exclusion. Under this method, European Union Member States would develop common objectives with respect to combatting social exclusion, monitor national progress in achieving them and engage in collective assessments of the results. The question of applying this method to pensions would be discussed under the forthcoming Belgian presidency. The speaker expressed strong agreement with statements in the Office report that social protection was an essential part of sustainable development. He also concurred with the Office report that the greatest challenge posed by ageing populations related not to social security but to national employment policy.

A representative speaking on behalf of Social Alert, the International Federation of University Women and Zonta International observed that social security was the right of every person, guaranteed in the United Nations International Covenant on Economic, Social and Cultural Rights (1966) as well as in a number of ILO Conventions. Social protection should be universal, comprehensive and based on the principle of solidarity. It should not be based on individual savings accounts where only those with stable revenues benefited and from which the great majority of low-paid workers in precarious employment were excluded. Equal access to social security should be provided to men and women. Any reform should aim for greater protection of women's rights and greater gender equality. Decent work provided the underpinning of any efficient and comprehensive social security system. It was the guarantor of sustainable human development. Governments, enterprises and workers must share the responsibility for good governance and meet the challenge of financing. Comprehensive coverage was a right of peoples and an obligation of States.

The Chairperson referred to the proposed reorganization of the points for discussion contained in document C.S.S./D.1. annexed (see p. 29) to this report. The Committee agreed to take the suggested six points as the basis for its discussion.

Point 1. Social security and economic development

Addressing the first point for discussion, the Worker Vice-Chairperson asserted the positive role of social security in enhancing change, improving living standards, and increasing the productivity of enterprises and economies. Social security contributed to social cohesion and labour productivity by maintaining the good health of the labour force, easing the departure of older workers, and making all workers better able to accept change. While the globalization of national economies was making social security more necessary than ever, it had also placed limits on States' abilities to finance this protection. Trade unionists were convinced that people wanted to see social security strengthened and that measures to achieve this would not interfere with economic growth.

The Employer Vice-Chairperson took issue with the notion that social security invariably contributed to economic growth. Rather, it depended on national circumstances and on the design and cost of a social security scheme. For example, while health insurance could be useful in improving living standards, it could also become prohibitively costly, as in the case of the AIDS pandemic. Such epidemics might strain health-care financing to the point that it would become necessary to target benefits through social assistance. If social security were well managed, it could enhance productivity; but if its costs were too high, it could have a negative impact on the competitiveness of firms and on employment levels.

The Chairperson recognized a series of Government members to address the first point for discussion. Many of them expressed their appreciation of the excellent Office report, which would greatly facilitate the work of the Committee. A number of them stated that there was no single model or formula for a successful social security scheme. Rather, schemes had to be structured to reflect national conditions; and they had to include flexible design features which allowed for continuing changes as new problems and challenges arose. One Government member compared his national scheme to a living organism which had grown and developed over time, first providing social assistance for the poor, then expanding to include social insurance for the workforce and finally evolving to a full-blown concept of social security for all complemented by supplementary schemes. Another member suggested the possibility of a cascade-type model for social security development with progressive steps. Each step would be designed to achieve some progress in extending social security coverage to a larger portion of the workforce. The stabilizing effect of social security was viewed as especially necessary in this era of globalization, since trade liberalization could cause social tensions to rise. Some members contended that modern democratic governments were unable to survive without strong systems of social security. Others held that social security could actually vitalize the economy by reducing workers' fears of economic change.

Several Government members stated that the positive effect of social security on productivity must be factored into consideration of its costs. One member said that these costs tended to be examined mainly in terms of their impact on enterprises in light of their costs at the microeconomic level, but when looked at from the macroeconomic level, they were simply a redistribution of income from workers to the inactive population. These social transfers were not a burden to the nation and did not hamper international competitiveness. Rather than being conceived of primarily in terms of cost, social security should be regarded as an investment, an agent for social cohesion and a national asset. As an investment, it contributed to the health of the population and improved the situations of families. At the same time, it had an anti-cyclical economic effect, maintaining consumer demand for goods and services during times of high unemployment. It also promoted labour mobility by allowing workers to move from job to job without the risk of losing earned entitlements. Its importance as a national asset was reflected in recent decisions by the European Court of Human Rights that citizens had a property right in social security, making it a source of income and wealth. Moreover, social security schemes redistributed income in a manner which maintained and reinforced the dignity of beneficiaries. This in turn contributed to social cohesion and national solidarity.

The Chairperson invited the Employer Vice-Chairperson to respond to the comments by Government members. He noted three themes in the interventions. First, he said, many Government members recognized that social security policy could not be considered in isolation. Rather, it was an integral part of a country's economic framework. Second, globalization created a need for new ideas, approaches and answers related to the structuring of social security. Third, social security could not be financed unless there were jobs, as the two were directly linked. He added that the concept of decent work may depend on the national context and that social security standards designed for industrialized countries may not bring about the intended results when applied in developing countries. For this reason, the ILO should focus more heavily on national, as opposed to international, approaches to social security provision.

The Worker Vice-Chairperson also described the themes he perceived in the Government members' interventions. He noted agreement among many Government members that social security enhanced social cohesion, improved the competitiveness of firms and economies and should be regarded as a national investment rather than an economic burden. He took issue with the Employer Vice-Chairperson's contention that decent work may depend on the national context, holding instead that the principles underlying decent work were the same regardless of country. Rather than relating to employment conditions, the concept of decent work was more about the fundamental rights of workers as provided in the ILO Conventions.

Point 2. Extension of social security coverage

Turning to the second point for discussion, the Chairperson gave the floor first to the Worker Vice-Chairperson who said that his group's highest priority was to extend social security coverage to excluded individuals and families. While micro-insurance schemes might contribute to this in a limited way, they were unlikely to provide a solution for large numbers of people. He supported further ILO development and research work on this approach to the extent that it showed potential for expansion and that such schemes could be integrated with national social security schemes. Another option which should be explored was the establishment of targeted schemes of social assistance, tailored to assist those most in need. From the workers' perspective, high priority should be given to measures, such as education and training, which enabled informal-sector workers to move into formal employment. The provision of social security cash payments could make such skills acquisition possible. The Workers' group also considered that a universal health-care system, financed through general revenue and if necessary supplementary contributions, constituted an essential part of social security.

The Employer Vice-Chairperson stated that extending social security coverage was a difficult challenge which could not be dealt with simplistically. The target population was heterogeneous, including the self-employed, small entrepreneurs and legal and illegal migrants. The excluded differed markedly in their needs, conditions of work and ability to make contributions, requiring tailored solutions which should be devised and implemented at the national level. The speaker considered that over time it might be possible to develop special systems for collecting contributions so that social security coverage could be extended to persons who were outside the formal economy. He commented that in some countries such workers were successfully resorting to microinsurance to cover health care and other risks. He described the situation of some workers who initially were obliged to work in the informal economy and later fell into the habit of not paying taxes or social security contributions. It was critically important to avoid placing an extra financial burden on employers and workers in the formal sector to finance benefits for the informal sector. The ILO should undertake detailed studies of different groups of excluded workers to serve as the basis for national policy development.

The Chairperson invited comments from Government members, many of whom expressed concern that the growth of informal employment was placing increasing numbers of workers beyond the reach of national social security schemes. In some developing countries, the informal economy was much larger than the formal one, creating enormous challenges for the extension of coverage. Several members agreed that the informal economy must not be regarded as a solution for the unemployed and underemployed, but rather as a re-entry point or a transition into formal employment. One member noted that it was much more difficult for developing countries than industrialized countries to finance the extension of social security to vulnerable categories of the population. Another stated that her country believed there should be a core minimum of protection for all; with the challenge of declining formal employment, her Government was experimenting with various types of taxation to finance this. A variety of approaches to extend social security were described by members from developing countries. One reported on an experiment in his country to extend coverage to some self-employed workers with low incomes, providing subsidized basic benefits in return for minimal contributions. Another, coming from a country in which the vast majority of the workforce was in the informal economy, referred to various social insurance and social assistance schemes established by central and state governments in order to extend coverage to numerous groups of the population. He mentioned a pilot initiative to bring social security coverage to a large sector of agricultural workers and also noted that microinsurance had achieved some success when linked with microcredit and self-help groups. A member from a country with an extensive social insurance system reported on recent legislation which provided a basic benefit to all persons over age 75 with no other income.

In some industrialized countries too, particularly the transition economies, similar problems were appearing with the movement of more and more workers into self-employment. Where existing schemes were designed to cover only employees, the question was arising whether or not to reform the basic pension system, by moving from a system of worker solidarity to one of national solidarity. One member said that there was universal social security coverage in her country, but that for the self-employed, notably those in agriculture, certain cash benefit schemes other than pensions were voluntary in character. Another member from an industrialized country noted the diversity of needs and circumstances in different countries and observed that her own had a universal means-tested social security system which contributed to poverty reduction and gender equality.

The Worker and Employer Vice-Chairpersons in turn expressed appreciation for these comments. The Employer Vice-Chairperson said that they revealed the dimensions of the problem and the complexities of extending coverage. He reiterated the need for greater flexibility in the design of social security schemes and for tax-based financing of coverage extensions, including the possibility of reliance on value added taxes. The Worker Vice-Chairperson also acknowledged the need for flexibility in scheme design but stressed this must be provided within the framework of generally respected principles. He was pleased to note that not a single Government member had said that the extension of social security was an impossible task. The idea that social security might not be affordable was unacceptable, in view of the amounts which governments were able to devote to military expenditure. He endorsed the view of the informal economy as a transition to formal employment. He concluded that proposals for extending coverage must be concrete and workable so as to avoid raising false hopes among excluded workers.

Point 3. Income security for the unemployed and employment

The Worker Vice-Chairperson observed that income security for the unemployed was a major challenge for countries at all levels of development. Not enough jobs had been created to stop increases in unemployment due to structural and technological changes, poor economic management and restrictive fiscal and monetary policies. Structural adjustment policies had increased unemployment in developing countries, and transition economies had seen massive increases as well. Around the world more than three-quarters of unemployed persons had no unemployment insurance.

Most unemployed workers who received benefits were in industrialized countries. There had, however, been a tendency to reduce unemployment benefits over the past decade on the pretext that the level of benefits discouraged people from seeking work. The Workers' group rejected this argument. Some countries with relatively generous benefits had low rates of unemployment, whereas some with low benefit levels had high unemployment.

Unemployment insurance schemes in developing countries had rather limited coverage. There the chief form of income maintenance consisted of labour-intensive infrastructure programmes which provided low-wage employment to otherwise unemployed persons. The Workers' group supported such initiatives in appropriate circumstances. Workers denounced World Bank policies which had actively opposed the establishment of unemployment insurance schemes in developing countries.

The Workers' group believed that a number of initiatives were needed to respond to the problem of increased unemployment and decreased income maintenance. First, policies restricting eligibility or benefit duration should be reversed. Second, international financial institutions must stop campaigning against unemployment insurance in middle-income developing countries and economies in transition. Third, state-guaranteed funds should ensure that, in the event of bankruptcy, dismissed workers received the lump-sum separation payments which were their due. Fourth, universal access to some basic services, such as health care, would ease the impact of unemployment. Fifth, programmes should be designed to reach unprotected workers in the informal economy in order to bring them into the formal economy. Finally, governments must ensure that resources were available to provide a sound education for all young people.

The speaker emphasized that the best means to ensure social protection and income security was a job. Access to employment was the ultimate aim. Vocational training and work experience should be made available to the unemployed to upgrade their skills and improve their chances of rapid re-employment. Infrastructure construction programmes should offer not just short-term employment but an opportunity to prepare for future work.

The Employer Vice-Chairperson stressed that the question of income security must be examined with care. It was important to situate the debate in terms of job loss in the formal sector. The first principle was that, in order to receive benefits, a worker who loses his or her job must have contributed to the system. A well-planned and well-managed system was only possible if funding was secure. This depended on adequate inputs. In some countries, however, people had become addicted to unemployment. High benefit levels encouraged this.

The overall economic environment had to be considered in devising an approach to deal with the problem of unemployment. There were enormous differences between industrialized, middle-income and developing countries, and economies in transition. Measures to respond to the problems raised by unemployment should be tailored to the circumstances of each country. Responses depended on national social policies and government budgets.

Insurance schemes were not the only answer to unemployment. In some cases, labour-intensive employment projects could provide jobs to ensure survival for those who would otherwise be unemployed. Ultimately, the problem of unemployment could be solved only by creating jobs and preparing unemployed workers to return to active working life. Individuals must recognize their obligation to society and prove themselves willing and able to look for work. Training should aim to prepare workers for the new jobs that society would need. Indeed, education, training and retraining were key to improving the quality of the workforce. Employers did not wish to lose good workers. On the contrary, they made great efforts to retain the best. Clearly, there was a need for improved training capacity to impart skills and there was a role for employers to play in training institutions.

A rich discussion ensued, as the representatives of many Governments contributed insights drawn from their own national experiences. It was clearly a challenge for legislators and policy-makers to devise the appropriate blend of policy options which would ensure a decent livelihood and quality employment for the workforce. There was wide consensus that income support measures alone were insufficient in terms of meeting the needs of the unemployed. Active employment policies were a necessary complement.

Systems of income support had several functions. They were needed to provide long-term benefits to those who had permanently left the labour force, for example due to disability, as well as short-term income replacement to those who were temporarily out of work due, for example, to unemployment or injury. Attending to the special needs of people with disabilities to encourage their re-entry into the workforce was also important. The use of sickness and accident programmes could contribute to this end. Families with children should be assisted through the provision of child allowances, and a minimum level of income should be assured to those without other sources of income or with very low incomes.

Unemployment benefits were an essential component of a comprehensive social security system but they could be difficult to design properly. A balance must be found in order to provide the necessary income replacement benefits to people who were out of work, while avoiding dependency on income support which might discourage the search for new employment. Unemployment insurance funds provided workers with greater income security but mechanisms had to be put in place to guard against abuse. Compliance with the payment of contributions was also a problem. The participation of the social partners in the design and monitoring of social security systems could contribute to their smooth functioning.

Besides their importance to individuals and families, one Government member noted that unemployment benefits played an important additional role in stabilizing the national economy, as funds were accumulated during periods of economic growth and expended during periods of economic contraction.

It was not possible to apply a "one-size-fits-all" approach to the development of unemployment insurance schemes. The circumstances of each country needed to be taken into account. In many developing countries, for example, where demands were high and resources limited, cash payments to the unemployed were considered unrealistic. Other approaches had to be devised to meet their needs.

A number of Government members mentioned the need for active labour market policies to help the unemployed. Job creation was fundamental. A wide consensus emerged that the best protection against unemployment was an active employment policy. It was not enough to give the means of subsistence to the unemployed; jobs had to be created. Active employment measures were an investment which could help countries stay competitive.

Financial institutions should implement policies that promoted job creation and economic growth. One Government member proposed linking direct foreign investment and employment creation. There was no single response to the problem of unemployment. To ensure decent work would require a multiple approach involving job creation, education, training and retraining.

The purpose of skills training programmes and vocational training opportunities was to facilitate the smooth transfer of labour from unemployment to re-employment. It was important to link training and retraining programmes with job creation efforts, so that people had jobs to go to after their training was completed. Retraining should be strategically targeted to present and future labour market needs. In order to achieve this, partnerships should be established between training institutions and national employment creation funds. Another option would be to involve well-established enterprises in tripartite or jointly managed programmes to encourage job creation.

New approaches were needed to provide training and retraining possibilities to the unemployed, including the uninsured. Training programmes had to be targeted to take into account the skills, experience and circumstances of the unemployed. An institution for skills assessment and demand-driven skills development training could be an effective means of encouraging re-employment. Traineeships could be of particular interest to young workers.

Developing the full potential of workers involved a number of essential components. It was important to consider additional literacy and numeracy training, especially in an age of labour migration. Lifelong learning was essential to keep up with changes in technology and to remain employable. Better development of human resources could positively affect labour mobility, making it possible to get the right people to where the jobs were.

Income support measures could be used to ease the transition from unemployment to re-employment. Several Government members described the strategies their Governments had used, which had contributed to a decline in unemployment. By maintaining some level of income support during training and after the initial return to work, these policies encouraged unemployed workers to take the risk of changing their current situations. The long-term unemployed could be encouraged to resume their education while receiving benefits. To encourage their return to work, unemployment benefits could be continued during the initial period of employment, but on a reducing scale. Those who entered self-employment could receive a portion of benefits during the start-up phase. One speaker noted the need for seed capital for these workers and urged the ILO to carry out more research on credit schemes which would lead to economic empowerment. If possible, supplemental health benefits should not be immediately withdrawn after the return to work. Other options which would help to "make work pay" included the provision of additional child benefits, the reduction of income tax rates, the introduction of a national minimum wage, and allowing part-time work for a spouse without a total loss of benefits when an income threshold had been reached.

Many speakers agreed that there was a need to share information on the policies and practices which could contribute to a smooth transition from unemployment to secure and decent work. Unemployment benefit schemes should be capable of securing at least the basic livelihood of displaced workers while they adapted to structural changes in the economy. Active labour market policies should stimulate re-employment through skills development and other incentives. Most importantly, jobs must be created to provide decent work to an ever-growing workforce.

Point 4. Equality between men and women

Turning to the fourth point for discussion, the Employer Vice-Chairperson stated that gender equality was of great importance for the healthy development of society. Equal treatment of men and women in social security was crucial in so far as universal schemes were concerned. However, the issue was more complex regarding schemes established by employers or where employers made contributions. In those cases, entitlement often depended on how long a person had worked or even how many hours per week. Women were probably at a disadvantage in this respect with regard to their pensions due to periods of absence related to family responsibilities. Nonetheless, that was an issue that should be left to national debate and any decision should take account of the impact on enterprises. It was not preferential treatment but equality that should be sought when considering regulations aimed at dealing with real or perceived discrimination. Any changes that might be suggested to these regulations should be discussed in light of fiscal spending priorities at the national level.

The Worker Vice-Chairperson strongly affirmed that social security should not simply guarantee equal treatment for men and women, but should go further to grant women an improved place in society. Measures should be taken to redress discriminatory outcomes and their impact on women. Measures aimed at equitable outcomes would take account of the cumulative impact of women's experiences, such as a lifetime of lower pay and career interruptions for maternity, childcare and elder care. Women received less education and training than men and were more likely to be engaged in part-time or casual work. Because of these factors, benefits based on employment clearly resulted in poorer outcomes for women. Women were also subject to cultural constraints that denied them access to financing, inheritance and property rights.

The Workers' group stressed the importance of equal pay for work of equal value. Men and women should both be paid the correct rate for the job. The introduction of a minimum wage was a major factor in lifting women from the low-pay poverty trap. Unfortunately, discrimination in pay systems and the fact that women were still more likely to be in low-wage employment impacted negatively on their pension entitlements. It was essential to include equal value strategies in social security systems. The right to social security needed to be an individual right which was not dependent on a spouse's entitlement. A basic entitlement was needed for each individual. There was a real need for positive action in a number of areas. Social security payments should be made during maternity leave and periods of childcare and elder care. Percentage links to pay should be re-examined, since they tended to disadvantage women. Social security Conventions should contain specific provisions stipulating that there must be no discrimination against women. There must be provision for family allowances. Adequate survivors' pensions needed to be developed. In cases of family break-up or divorce, equity in benefits splitting should take into account who provided care for dependants. Family-friendly workplaces, childcare and elder care facilities and other forms of social infrastructure were important as well. In conclusion, it was suggested that all policy proposals for social security schemes should be subject to gender analysis and that a stringent monitoring process should be developed to ensure that social security schemes did not lead to discriminatory outcomes.

A great number of Government members affirmed the principle of equal treatment for women and men, considering it to be an explicit goal in social security reform. One Government member observed that the social security system in his country drew no distinction between men and women in terms of retirement age, social security eligibility requirements and benefit amounts, and payment of survivor and dependant benefits. Another noted that in his country, the Government and employers made contributions without discrimination based on sex and contributions were deducted from men's and women's salaries on an equal basis. Several Government members noted the fact that even where systems were designed to provide equal treatment, discrimination persisted due to differential wage rates for men and women. Where social security benefits were earnings-based, women contributed less and also received less upon retirement.

Many Government members also supported the view that equality of treatment alone was insufficient in a number of respects. The economic interests of women needed to be more fully safeguarded, and this could require positive measures to overcome discriminatory outcomes. Equal pay for work of equal value was crucial. Active labour market policies should include job creation for women and support measures to ensure sustained participation in the workforce, so that women's individual social security entitlements could rise. In even broader terms, gender equality included questions of education and access to health care. Raising awareness on equality of treatment for men and women was necessary. Women in particular should have adequate information in order to make informed choices. Incentives were needed to promote girls' access to education so that girls would have an equal chance to prepare themselves for the world of work. Social security was an important tool to advance gender equality, but it had to be recognized that men's and women's life cycles and needs were different. The provision of quality childcare was important in the framework of social protection, as was the issue of parental leave provided for both men and women to take time off to care for children. Child benefits were a high priority. Specific policy responses were necessary to enable workers to balance work and family life without encountering systemic discrimination. Affordable childcare could play an important role in ensuring the sustained participation of women in the labour market, thus increasing their entitlement to benefits, which in most social security systems were linked to gainful employment.

One Government member explained his country's "passive approach" towards ensuring women's entitlements were not compromised by periods of non-employment due to family responsibilities. When retirement benefits were calculated, those periods when women were caring for young children, and therefore not engaged in full-time employment, were not considered. The average income calculations were therefore not affected by extended periods of low or no income. Alternatively, the "active approach" adopted by some governments gave women credit for periods when their earning capacity was significantly lower so as not to compromise women's entitlement to benefits in the long term. This approach could create entitlements for women who otherwise might have none.

One of the most important reform measures cited by a number of Government members was to base tax and benefit systems on individual rather than derived rights. The shift from derived to individualized rights was not easy, but tax and benefit systems could provide strong incentives for women to enter and stay in the labour market. One Government member saw gender equality in social security as an important precondition for higher employment rates and thus for economic growth.

Two Government members noted that sex-differentiated annuity rates made distinctions based on the different life expectancies of men and women — to the detriment of women. To counter discriminatory outcomes based on life expectancy, one Government member described his country's recent reform requiring the use of unisex actuarial tables, which resulted in higher pension payments for women than under the previous sex-disaggregated system. Changes in his country's employment law had also served to reduce discrimination against women workers. For example, employers who hired women with children paid a lower social security contribution. This encouraged employers to hire more working mothers. Several initiatives had improved social security coverage for workers engaged in flexible forms of employment, most notably domestic workers, of whom the overwhelming majority were women.

Research was needed in several areas to understand better how discriminatory outcomes were produced. Pension splitting might be one way to reduce discrimination based on dependency. It was also important to examine why benefit differentials continued to exist even with regard to women who had uninterrupted employment histories.

Survivors' benefits and pensions were an issue requiring much fuller examination. Most schemes were rooted in the concept of dependency and survivors' need for a replacement income. The concept of survivors' pensions was considered problematic in more than one country. Where possible, it might be worthwhile to develop bridging mechanisms to assist survivors in adjusting to their new life circumstances, for example, in their return to employment once their children had become independent. Of course, in the case of older survivors without previous employment experience, self-sufficiency through work was unlikely. It was important that all solutions be humane. A number of Governments were studying the issue of survivors' pensions critically.

A number of Government members described in some detail specific social security programmes which provided assistance to women. These included monthly allowances for pregnant women, maternity leave and benefits, child benefits, allowances for single women over 50 years of age, early retirement plans, pension payments to women who left the workforce to raise children, and support payments to divorced women, widows and orphans.

Many Government members expressed the desire to learn more about the best practices in other countries. Committee discussions had already highlighted a number of positive initiatives and experiences from which member States could learn. The documentation and distribution of information on best practices was seen as essential for achieving progress at the national and international levels.

One Government member stated that, while systems had to be flexible, they should also be rooted in a strong framework of international standards as formulated by the ILO. In terms of gender equality issues, however, many speakers considered the Social Security (Minimum Standards) Convention, 1952 (No. 102), to be outdated. It was based on the male breadwinner/female homemaker model which did not take adequate account of women's labour market participation. Such a model no longer provided an efficient basis for the distribution of benefits.

The Worker Vice-Chairperson summarized the main views of the Workers' group concerning gender equality. Clearly there was systemic discrimination against women in social security systems. The Workers' group were pleased that a number of Government members had seen the need to go beyond merely guaranteeing equal treatment of women in social security systems and to apply other measures to promote gender equality. The achievement of equitable treatment could require positive discrimination in some areas. The individualization of pension rights was a vital issue for the Workers' group. Reconciliation of work and family life was also important. The speaker noted that Convention No. 102 had been written as though men were the social security recipients and women merely their dependants, and although it contained important principles, this aspect caused concern. An important issue which had not yet been discussed was the need for social security systems to address gender aspects of the HIV/AIDS pandemic. Mothers were being faced with additional responsibilities of supporting and raising their young children alone when their husbands died, and older women were having to care for entire families of orphans as the parents died.

The Employer Vice-Chairperson expressed the Employers' group's keen interest in the lively debate that had taken place. He focused attention on the language being used in the discussions. Terms such as "equal treatment" and "discrimination" could mean different things in different languages or societies, and did not necessarily refer to gender-based sources of discrimination. Many factors needed to be taken into consideration. Gender equality was only one of those. This was one reason why such matters should be dealt with at the national level. Many problems concerning gender equality were unrelated to social security. Problems related to pensions and women's biological functions needed to be solved at the national level. The ILO should certainly work to find solutions for the challenges facing member States and to provide technical assistance to countries that requested it to redress the discrimination that women still faced in the labour market. The speaker concurred that Convention No. 102 was a "dinosaur", representing the macho man as the sole provider. Such a view was out of date in 2001. Social security was a matter that concerned society at large. Each member of society had to play a part in seeking an adequate solution to the problems of inequality and discrimination. Social dialogue and the collective-bargaining process could contribute to the search for solutions, taking into account the capacity and resources of enterprises. The Employers' group were ready to work with governments in order to seek financially feasible solutions, which could be developed in consensus with the social partners.

Point 5. Financing of social security and ageing

Turning to the fifth point for discussion, the Employer Vice-Chairperson expressed two reservations about the Office report. First, the report did not assign sufficient importance to the problem of demographic ageing. While the elderly generally made up a smaller portion of the populations of developing countries than of industrialized countries, demographic studies suggested that developing countries would age at faster rates. Second, the report might have been premature in concluding that measures to increase employment were the most useful means of containing pension costs as national populations grew older. More research was needed on other policy options, especially increased reliance on private pension provision. The optimal pension system might turn out to be a mixed one in which the State provided minimum benefits and relied on private funds for supplementation. More research was also needed on the impact of HIV/AIDS on pay-as-you-go pension schemes.

The Worker Vice-Chairperson expressed agreement with the Office report that higher employment was key to strengthening the financing of social security in ageing societies. Workers were ready to engage in social dialogue on a number of options to help achieve this, including training to update the skills of older workers and measures to encourage gradual retirement. In addition, the substantial military budgets of many governments indicated that they could spend more on social security or could shift budgetary revenues to this purpose. In many countries, the World Bank had advocated privatization and pre-funding of pensions as a means of averting an "old-age crisis" in social security financing. However, this had proven ineffective and had produced many new problems. These included high administrative charges for private pension management, in the region of 25 per cent of a worker's lifetime contributions; high government expenditures on pension supervision and some costly bailouts; high transitional costs, incurred to meet current benefit commitments while building up reserves for a new pre-funded scheme; and great inequality in private benefits paid to workers with similar amounts of savings, resulting from volatility in the financial markets where these savings were invested. The Worker Vice-Chairperson reiterated his support for the governing principles of pension schemes discussed at the Committee's first sitting. Recalling that social security concerned much more than pensions, he urged that high priority be placed on finding new approaches to extending the coverage of public schemes, especially for health care.

Government members expressed differing opinions on whether changes in pension financing were needed to deal with national ageing, in particular with the rise in life expectancy. On one side, several members asserted that a shift from pay-as-you-go financing to pre-funding of pensions could be useful. Under some circumstances, it could help to increase national savings and lead to higher rates of economic growth. This would make it easier for countries to bear the increased burden of financing pensions for an ageing population. At the same time, this shift to pre-funding would place new demands on governments. They would have to regulate pension management firms to ensure that they did not discriminate against low-income workers and that they placed workers' financial interests ahead of their own. Moreover, no matter what form of financing was chosen, government would have to remain the ultimate guarantor of the system. Several Government members cited risk diversification as an additional rationale for a move to pre-funding. They held that since pay-as-you-go financing was vulnerable to demographic ageing and pre-funding was vulnerable to poor economic performance, a mixed system which incorporated both approaches could afford workers a measure of protection against both risks. Defined benefits within a pay-as-you-go scheme could be financed in part through a scheme reserve fund, which would make it possible to soften the effects of sharp demographic changes.

Other Government members took a different view, arguing that a shift in the method of financing pensions would not in itself alter the economic burden that a country must bear to support its elderly. Unlike individual savers who could put extra resources away in anticipation of a large expenditure, nations were unable to save in advance to support a larger retired population. Rather, all pension systems, whether pay-as-you-go, pre-funded or a combination of these, were mechanisms for dividing current national income between active and retired workers. Pay-as-you-go pension schemes made this transfer of current income in a transparent way, but it was just as real in pre-funded systems. Following this logic, several members challenged the claim that pre-funded systems were superior to pay-as-you-go under conditions of demographic ageing. They argued that ageing affected funded systems in an indirect but equally significant way, namely through reducing the number of active workers who could purchase the private investments of the retiring population. This would in turn cause a drop in the value of their accumulated private savings. Several Government members also expressed concerns about the risks of prefunding and insisted on the need for prudence. One pointed out that his country had originally established a pre-funded pension system but had converted it to pay-as-you-go due to the unanticipated effects of inflation and war in depleting its financial reserves. He also stressed the risk of financial speculation and the potential for asset prices to fall around 2030, when large numbers of persons with pension savings accounts would have retired. The risk would grow in relation to the portion of benefits paid through funded schemes. Concerns were also expressed about high administrative costs of private pension management and about high volatility in the value of worker savings in existing private schemes. Citing these arguments, several Government members stated that they were not planning to change their method of financing pensions in anticipation of demographic ageing. They instead concurred with the Office report that increasing labour force participation offered the best approach to the problem, and they described several recent initiatives to encourage older workers to remain in the labour force. These included promoting part-time work and more flexible working hours, instituting programmes of vocational retraining and lifelong learning, reducing social contributions for older workers and encouraging firms to retain their employees beyond normal retirement age. In addition, several Government members stressed the importance of tripartite structures for social dialogue as a means of reaching consensus on reforms to deal with the costs related to ageing. Ways were also described to increase efficiency in the collection of contributions: create incentives for employers and workers to pay their contributions; inspire confidence that contributions to social security were used for the proper purpose; and simplify administrative formalities, for example, through the classic method of deduction from salary of the unified processing of contributions to all branches of social security.

Several Government members representing African countries stated that national ageing was far less of a problem for their social security schemes than was HIV/AIDS. This pandemic was putting pressure on scheme financing and threatening the very existence of some pension funds. One Government member said that his country was experiencing similar problems due to resistant strains of malaria. There was a pressing need for research on the implications of these diseases, particularly HIV/AIDS, for the financing of social security.

The Worker Vice-Chairperson expressed appreciation for several comments made by Government members. These related to the need to preserve and strengthen public pension schemes, to extend their coverage and to increase employment and economic growth as the best means of containing pension financing costs as populations age. He also concurred that, whatever form of pension scheme was chosen, government must serve as its ultimate guarantor.

The Employer Vice-Chairperson concluded that all types of social security financing had their strengths and weaknesses. The challenge was to find the system which best matched national conditions, needs and preferences. While agreeing with the Worker Vice-Chairperson that government had a key role to play in whatever type of system was chosen, he also held that the social partners should be closely involved in scheme governance. He called for increased international cooperation in the search for workable solutions to the problems associated with demographic ageing.

Point 6. Social dialogue and ILO activities

The Chairperson turned to the final point of discussion on tripartism and improvements in social security, long-term priorities for ILO work on social security and the possible application of the integrated approach to standard setting in the field of social security. The Employer Vice-Chairperson stressed that national realities differed widely. Hence, each country needed to find its own solutions based on its own circumstances. Through social dialogue, governments and organizations of employers and of workers could create social consensus and the political will to act. Tripartism was the basis of good governance and efficiency. The ILO should strengthen the capacity of the social partners to engage in tripartite and joint discussions and inform Members of the best methods of social dialogue. There was wide scope for further research by the ILO as various themes had emerged from the Committee's discussions. The benefits of interactions with other organizations such as the World Bank and the International Monetary Fund (IMF) had to be considered. Specifically, research needed to show what systems had worked and why. Two interesting themes which merited further work were reinsurance in the field of social protection, and health care for the poor. Social security was not free. It involved costs for society and particularly for employers and workers. It was important to understand how financing systems worked in order to achieve the right balance among competing interests and to avoid costs which impaired competitiveness. Good governance and low administration costs were essential. Other themes for further research included demographic questions, gender and discrimination, the interaction of social security and the labour market and their impact on the national economy and enterprises, various aspects of the informal economy and the relevance of ILO standards on social security. More work in these areas could be done, in the view of the Employers' group, through meetings of technical experts, supported by in-depth, quality research in order to have more complete and focused discussion on these issues in particular. These proposals provided sufficient work for the next ten to 15 years.

The Worker Vice-Chairperson observed that no social security system could function efficiently without the confidence of the people who participated in the system. Systemic discrimination against specific groups, such as women workers and migrants, had to be overcome. Institutionalized representation and, in particular, tripartite oversight and governance had proven helpful in creating consensus-based governance systems responsive to the changing needs of the global economy. The Workers' group called on governments to create a regulatory framework that encouraged tripartite consultations. Social security was seen as a valuable policy instrument to assist workers to move from unprotected work to decent work. If social security was to be sustainable, the growth of the informal economy had to be reversed. Initiatives of informal workers to organize themselves and to build formal institutions to provide social protection should be supported. The ILO should base its future activities on the concept of decent work and the values laid down in international labour standards on social security, namely the Social Security (Minimum Standards) Convention, 1952 (No. 102), the Equality of Treatment (Social Security) Convention, 1962 (No. 118), the Employment Injury Benefits Convention, 1964 [Schedule I amended in 1980] (No. 121), the Invalidity, Old-Age and Survivors' Benefits Convention, 1967 (No. 128), the Medical Care and Sickness Benefits Convention, 1969 (No. 130), the Maintenance of Social Security Rights Convention, 1982 (No. 157), the Employment Promotion and Protection against Unemployment Convention, 1988 (No. 168), and the Maternity Protection Convention, 2000 (No. 183). Key principles to be adopted by the ILO included recognizing social security as a universal right; endorsing its value for social equity, social stability, economic development and change as well as its capacity to provide universal benefits. The speaker urged the ILO to undertake research and technical cooperation in the areas of comprehensive financing and governance of social security schemes, the extension of coverage to the unprotected and ways to eradicate discriminatory outcomes. As an overall objective, the ILO should commit itself to a ten-year plan to achieve major improvements in social security for the excluded majority. The ILO would thus strengthen its role as a principal international institution in the area of social security. The speaker believed that the existing Conventions provided a good framework to define the basic principles of social security. Their further ratification should be promoted. With regard to the integrated approach, the results of the pilot exercise in the field of occupational health and safety should be evaluated before embarking on any further standard setting.

A number of Government members supported the view that tripartite collaboration and social dialogue could contribute to the development of effective social security systems well-adapted to local realities. Indeed, the success of reform could depend on consensus among the social partners and wide social acceptance. Governments could not deal with social security on their own. For employers, social security represented an investment and for workers it ensured stability of income. Tripartite effort was necessary and should be tailored to each country's situation.

One Government member cited his Government's experience of tripartite consultation in the reform of its contributory pension scheme, which had been carried out in response to changing social and demographic trends. Another suggested that the tripartite management of social security schemes be strengthened. Because of the huge financial resources involved, all the social partners needed to be involved. Yet another spoke of the need to legislate for tripartite structures to ensure that these structures were functional. Tripartism should be extended to the grass-roots level. In order to ensure good governance, the social partners had to exercise mandates based on democratic principles.

One Government member noted that social dialogue was useful, but was not always effective. Governments should push ahead on important issues like extending coverage, and not take tripartite dialogue as a sine qua non for effective action. Another urged that thought be given to whether the ILO tripartite structure was capable of dealing with the problems of exclusion or whether the system needed to be revised.

One Government member observed that social security systems were effective only where there was expanded social dialogue and a sense of accountability. The active participation of social partners was needed to extend social security services, but experience in her country had demonstrated the need to include NGOs, cooperatives and local governments as well.

With regard to the future activities of the ILO, many Government members offered concrete suggestions regarding research and technical cooperation activities. Among the particular problems and issues which should be reflected in both of these means of action were the following: the extension of coverage; the enhancement of good governance and resource management; the impact of globalization on developing countries' social security systems; the promotion of gender equality; appropriate responses to the HIV/AIDS pandemic, discrimination and social equity; better health and vocational rehabilitation of persons with disabilities; increasing the average retirement age; and improving conditions for older workers.

One Government member suggested that the primary focus of the ILO social security programme should be research and technical assistance regarding best practices for public and private social security schemes so as to support the goal of decent work. Others expressed the need for the ILO to develop the tools necessary to improve the coverage, design and governance of social security schemes and social protection policies. Indicators should be developed to measure the level of benefits and the degree of coverage and to serve as benchmarks of performance.

The ILO should offer technical assistance to developing countries via multidisciplinary teams to help reform and enhance social security systems, particularly as regards the large majority of excluded workers, but also in regard to training, investment schemes and risk management. An early warning system should be developed to identify crises in social security systems before they occurred. The ILO should also promote effective social dialogue in developing countries through technical cooperation.

A variety of pilot schemes were proposed by several Government members. These might include pilot projects in areas such as welfare funds for target groups in specific industries, insurance and pension schemes for agricultural workers, and state-promoted microinsurance schemes. Successful pilot schemes for workers in the informal economy should be documented and replicable models, which could be adapted to different situations, should be developed. Appropriate models would also be helpful for countries wishing to move from one type of system to another.

Turning to the question of standard setting, several Government members expressed the view that legally binding minimum standards should be an important part of the ILO strategy to assist countries in improving their social security coverage. Promoting the ratification of key social security standards or at least respect for the basic principles of those standards was crucial, particularly at a time when globalization was raising delicate issues of social protection.

Low ratification of ILO social security Conventions was not encouraging. Several Government members suggested that priority be given to rationalizing existing instruments, including Convention No. 102. In the view of one Government member, current standards were too detailed, difficult for non-experts to understand and too reliant on statistics which in many cases were unavailable. Further, they did not adequately reflect the role of women in the labour market. Several Government members preferred any new instruments to be limited to broad principles and be flexible enough to achieve wide ratification and implementation in different national situations. The exact mechanisms of implementation should be left to national law and practice. More flexible Conventions would enable more countries to participate in the ILO's standard-setting work.

More than one Government member found it unrealistic to consider the adoption of any monolithic social security Convention at the present time. Much more thinking was needed in order to develop a comprehensive approach to social security standards, particularly in light of the growing number of informal, unorganized and unprotected workers.

For another Government member, there was no need to revisit existing standards or to establish new ones. Existing standards should be taken into account by countries as they considered appropriate to their particular economic circumstances and their citizens' preferences.

Support for an integrated approach to standard setting was expressed by several Government members. Such an approach should be based on a detailed analysis of existing standards and, as expressed by one Government member, centred on human and social values. One Government member preferred to await completion of the current pilot experience before extending the integrated approach to social security.

The Employer Vice-Chairperson asserted that the Employers' group supported the efforts of the Governing Body concerning the revision of standards and the integrated approach to standard setting. He expressed pleasure at the convergence of views expressed within the Committee regarding the problems facing social security and potential solutions to be explored in the course of future work.

The Worker Vice-Chairperson noted the Government members' positive support for tripartism. Concerning the possible revision of standards, he drew members' attention to the fact that the Governing Body had found the existing standards to be relevant and sufficiently flexible to be adapted to different situations. ILO social security standards deserved ratification. Providing unprotected workers with access to social security was an immense challenge. It required an ambitious agenda of work for the ILO community. The Workers' group strongly urged the Committee to adopt a set of ambitious conclusions, which would advance the cause of providing social security to all.

Appendix

Reorganization of suggested points for discussion

In order to facilitate the general discussion, the representative of the Secretary-General proposes the following reorganization of the suggested points for discussion which were appended to Report VI. Essentially the points are similar; they have simply been grouped together by theme to take account of the fact that they will all have to be covered by the end of the sixth sitting of the Committee. For the convenience of delegates, the numbers of the original points which have been subsumed in each of the six themes are indicated in brackets.

1. The overall objective of social security is to provide income security and access to health care and as such it has an important role in achieving the goal of decent work. While some analyses indicate that the changing global context makes it more difficult to extend social security provision, others indicate that strong social security systems are necessary to sustain dynamic labour markets, achieve a more competitive economy and protect the population against economic instability. Does the provision of social security enhance the process of change, improve living standards and increase the productivity of enterprises and economies? (1, 4, 10)

2. Social protection coverage is often problematic in small workplaces, among the self-employed, among migrants and in the informal economy. Are there specific instruments and policies, for example microinsurance, that need to be put in place in order to address these problems and how can these responses contribute to bringing workers into the formal economy? (3)

3. What is the best means of providing income security to the unemployed and combining this with access to employment, at different levels of development and industrialization? (5)

4. Is it sufficient to guarantee equal treatment of women in social security schemes or do more specific measures need to be applied to ensure that social protection policies contribute to the promotion of gender equality? (6)

5. (i) Are changes to systems for financing old-age pensions or other policy measures necessary in order to meet the challenges of ageing populations faced by many countries? (7)

(ii) What are the advantages and disadvantages of alternative methods of financing social security, taking into account differences in ability to contribute to social insurance systems? Can private provision ease the financing of social security without undermining solidarity and universality? (8)

6. (i) How can ILO member States and the social partners work through the use of tripartism to ensure that the right to adequate social security and its good governance becomes a reality, including for those who presently are not covered? (2, 9)

(ii) What should be the long-term priorities for the ILO's research, standard-setting and technical assistance work in the social security field which will contribute to the overall goal of decent work? (11)

(iii) Taking into account the integrated approach to standard setting approved by the Governing Body in November 2000, how should this new approach be applied in the social security field? (12)

Social security: Issues, challenges and prospects Report VI to the International Labour Conference, 89th Session, 2001

Introduction

In 1999 the Governing Body of the International Labour Office decided that a general discussion on social security should take place at the International Labour Conference in 2001. The objective of this discussion is to establish an ILO vision of social security that, while continuing to be rooted in the basic principles of the ILO, responds to the new issues and challenges facing social security. In a second stage this may lead to the development of new instruments or to the possible updating or revision of existing standards.[1]

During the last two decades specific aspects of social security have been discussed at the International Labour Conference on various occasions. Most recently, in 2000, the Conference looked closely at the subject of maternity benefits when it revised the Maternity Protection Convention (Revised), 1952 (No. 103), and Recommendation (No. 95). Unemployment benefits were on the agenda in 1987 and 1988 when the Employment Promotion and Protection against Unemployment Convention, 1988 (No. 168), was discussed and adopted. In 1987 the Social Security (Seafarers) Convention (Revised) (No. 165) was adopted. The special needs of migrants were taken into account with the adoption in 1982 of the Maintenance of Social Security Rights Convention (No. 157).

However, it was in the 1950s — with the adoption in 1952 of the Social Security (Minimum Standards) Convention (No. 102) — and the 1960s — with the adoption of a series of superior standards — that the Conference dealt with the broad range of benefits provided by social security.

The last opportunity that the Conference had to consider social security as a whole was at the 80th Session in 1993 in the discussion of the Report of the Director-General, *Social insurance and social protection*. That discussion confirmed the bleak picture concerning the developing countries painted in the Report. The unfavourable situation of women with regard to social protection was emphasized,

---

[1] See ILO: Governing Body document GB.274/3, 274th Session, Geneva, March 1999.

as was the social distress which had resulted from structural adjustment policies. Some delegates had found the Report's analysis too optimistic with respect to the industrialized countries, noting that social protection was deteriorating, very often at the expense of the most vulnerable groups of the population. The social problems in the economies in transition were stressed: to ensure a smooth economic transformation and the development of democracy, it was vital to strengthen social protection. Many spoke about the relationship between economic growth and social protection, but it was clear that views differed considerably on this subject.

The Governing Body has identified a number of key issues that should be taken into account in the general discussion in 2001. These include: the interconnections between social security, employment and development; extension of the personal coverage of social protection; gender equality; the financing of social security; expanding social dialogue; and implications for future ILO work.[2] In this report a chapter is devoted to each of these topics. The report begins by looking at the global context in which social security schemes are now operating and the relevance of social security to the goal of decent work.

---

[2] For a more detailed discussion of these and other issues concerning social security, see ILO: *World Labour Report 2000: Income security and social protection in a changing world* (Geneva, 2000).

Chapter I

The prospects for social security

In many parts of the world, in the closing years of the twentieth century, social security systems have been under challenge. Some consider that the systems are too expensive, and that they harm the process of economic growth and development. Others point to deficiencies in the level of protection and the scope of coverage, and argue that in times of increased unemployment and other forms of labour insecurity, social security is more needed than ever. Particularly in the industrialized countries (including the transition economies of Central and Eastern Europe), social security systems must respond to new demographic challenges, such as ageing and changing family structures, with important implications for the financing of social protection. In some countries, there is dissatisfaction with the administration of social security, and calls for reform involve a review of the role of the State, the responsibilities of the social partners and the desirability of greater participation of the private sector.

One of the key global problems facing social security today is the fact that more than half of the world's population (workers and their dependants) is excluded from any type of social security protection. They are covered neither by a contribution-based social insurance scheme nor by tax-financed social benefits, while a significant additional proportion are covered for only a few contingencies. In sub-Saharan Africa and South Asia, statutory social security personal coverage is estimated at 5 to 10 per cent of the working population and in some cases is decreasing. In Latin America, coverage lies roughly between 10 and 80 per cent, and is mainly stagnating. In South-East and East Asia, coverage can vary between 10 and almost 100 per cent, and in many cases was until recently increasing. In most industrialized countries, coverage is close to 100 per cent, although in a number of these countries, especially those in transition, compliance rates have fallen in recent years.

In most of its standard-setting and technical cooperation activities on social security, the ILO had expected that an increasing proportion of the labour force in developing countries would end up in formal-sector employment or self-employment covered by social security. It implicitly assumed that past economic and social development patterns of the industrialized countries would replicate themselves in other regions. However, experience in developing countries — and more recently in the industrialized countries — has shown that this proportion is in many cases now stagnating or declining. Even in countries with high economic growth, increasing numbers of workers — often women — are in less secure employment, such as casual labour, home work and certain types of self-employment.

The growth of informal, unprotected work creates dangers for formal and informal economy workers alike. The area of social protection illustrates the very real and direct interest, on the part of workers with "normal" employment status and of their organizations, in bringing informal economy workers into the mainstream of formal employment. With shrinking formal employment, workers bear an increasing direct burden of financing social needs, with adverse effects on their quality of life. That burden may also undermine the capacity of enterprises to compete in the global economy.

The global context

Globalization, either alone or in combination with technological change, often exposes societies to greater income insecurity. Research on the developed countries suggests that income transfers tend to be largest in economies that are simultaneously very open and subject to substantial price risk in world markets. Other observers claim that reductions in income security and social protection arise from the attempts of governments to promote competitiveness and attract foreign direct investment. Some of them also foresee that tax competition will lead to further reductions in taxes, particularly on returns to capital, and lower the ability of governments to finance social protection.

The structural adjustment policies pursued in most developing countries have often contributed to a decline in the small percentage of the working population in the formal sector. The successive waves of structural adjustment programmes have also led to wage cuts in the public and private sectors, thereby eroding the financial base of statutory social insurance schemes. Simultaneously, many such schemes in developing countries have suffered from bad management and bad governance, which have often strongly reduced the trust of their members. In addition, structural adjustment programmes have often resulted in severe cuts in social budgets. In Benin, for example, health expenditure's share in the total government budget dropped from 8.8 to 3.3 per cent between 1987 and 1992. As most governments can no longer guarantee access to free health and education, there is — apart from national systems — greater demand for international and local arrangements to finance and organize these social services.

Particularly in low-income countries, structural adjustment and socio-economic changes have also produced large vulnerable groups that cannot contribute to social insurance schemes. The most vulnerable groups outside the labour force are people with disabilities and old people who cannot count on family support, and who have not been able to make provisions for their own pensions. Some countries, such as China and India, have taken specific social assistance measures to meet the needs of these groups.

The world today also faces a large number of complex crises, often with global repercussions. One of the most visible recent examples has been the Asian financial crisis, which led to massive job losses in the formal sector of the economy, rapidly rising unemployment, and an expansion of employment in the informal economy. Then there have been many armed conflicts in recent years, particularly in sub-Saharan Africa (Angola, Congo, Liberia and Rwanda, for example) but also in Europe (Bosnia and Herzegovina, Kosovo). Numerous countries around the world continue to be afflicted by health disasters, such as the HIV/AIDS pandemic, leaving many children orphans (see box). Natural disasters, such as recurrent droughts and floods (in Africa and Asia), earthquakes and hurricanes (for example in Turkey and Central America) have not only left many communities without homes and sources of income but have also wiped away years of their countries' efforts at development. Lastly, some countries are facing the difficult process of making economic as well as political transitions, whether from a centrally planned economy to a market-oriented system, or from a politically restrictive regime like apartheid to a multiracial and democratic society.

The challenge of HIV/AIDS for social security

The HIV/AIDS pandemic is the most dramatic of the challenges facing social security in certain countries, notably in Africa. Its human consequences are becoming all too evident, but its implications for social security systems are still far from fully known or understood.

The pandemic has served to underline the gravely inadequate nature of social protection systems in the countries most affected. Many of the indi- viduals who have been infected have no social security coverage. As a result they typically do not have access to the quality medical care they require. Nor — if they are breadwinners — do their dependants receive any replacement income when they die or become unable to carry on working. The first figure shows how dramatic the situation already is in many African countries.

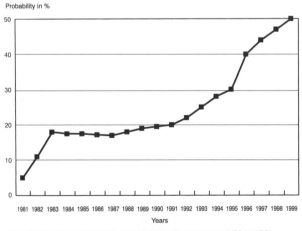

Probability of a 15-year-old boy dying before age 50, Zimbabwe

Probability in %

Years

Source: Estimates based on data from the Joint United Nations Programme on HIV/AIDS (UNAIDS),
at http://www.unaids.org/epidemic_update/report/epi_ext/sld019.htm.

In a typical African country, Zimbabwe, a 15-year-old boy today has only about a 50 per cent chance of reaching age 50. The equivalent figures for women are not available but it is to be expected that the pattern is not very different. That means implicitly that a huge number of families will lose their prime-age breadwinners before the pandemic can be halted.

The informal social protection mechanisms (extended family, local community) are being stretched well beyond breaking point by the large numbers of adult breadwinners now being struck down in their prime. Never was it more clear why social solidarity and risk-pooling must be organized on the widest possible basis: this is vital in order to ensure that all the necessary help is channelled to the family, groups, communities and regions most direly affected.

International solidarity is urgently needed to back up national efforts —

particularly to help in prevention campaigns and to assist in the provision of health care. Partnerships must be developed between the competent health authorities, governmental and non-governmental organizations and the drug industry to ensure a supply of medication which, if international prices were charged, would be totally beyond the reach of patients in certain communities. At the local level, social security schemes, health-care providers and social services must coordinate their efforts in order that AIDS sufferers receive proper care in the most appropriate setting.

The finances of social security schemes are being affected in a number of ways by the pandemic. Generally, their resource base declines with the general contraction that the AIDS pandemic inflicts on national economies. The second figure shows the estimated effect of AIDS on the Kenyan gross domestic product (GDP).

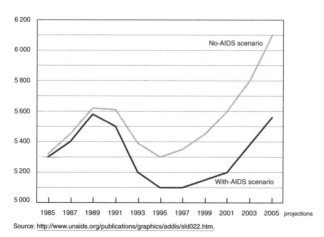

Estimated change in per capita GDP caused by AIDS, Kenya (in 1985 Kenyan shillings)

Source: http://www.unaids.org/publications/graphics/addis/sld022.htm.

In the industrialized countries, the financial impact of HIV/AIDS is much less serious; in the United States, for example, spending on HIV/AIDS care represents less than 1 per cent of personal health-care expenditure and the average cost of care per person is less than that of treating many other disabling conditions. However, the financial effects on individuals are often dramatic, particularly if they do not have adequate health insurance. In the United States, only 32 per cent of people with HIV have private health insurance (compared with 71 per cent of Americans overall); almost 50 per cent depend on Medicaid or Medicare for coverage; and about 20 per cent are uninsured. Even among people who have resources, the costs of HIV/AIDS care (approximately US$ 20,000 per annum per patient) can quickly exhaust their assets and leave them impoverished.[1] In most other industrialized countries, social security health-care systems or national health services protect people from this risk.

In many countries social security schemes will cease or have already ceased to receive contributions from workers who are unable to carry on working. Depending on the scope of the scheme, they are having to finance considerably higher expenditure on medical care, cash sickness benefits, disability benefits and, ultimately, survivors' benefits. Premature mortality, on the other hand, will tend to reduce expenditure on old-age pensions, but these savings will become significant only at a much later stage. Research is necessary to obtain the data that are indispensable for making valid projections and thereby to ensure the financial equilibrium of social security schemes in the long term. As part of its action against HIV/AIDS, the ILO is embarking on a project which seeks to assess the impact of AIDS on the financial viability of social insurance schemes and national budgets.[2]

Employers' and workers' organizations have an enormously important role to play in dealing with the pandemic. The workplace is a setting in which highly effective preventive activities can be conducted. Investment in such activities pays off handsomely by helping to retain a healthy and experienced workforce and to contain the costs of employer medical care, sick pay and pension schemes. Companies can maximize the benefits of their prevention activities by involving not only their employees, but also their clients and the community of which they are a part.

---

[1] Kaiser Family Foundation: "Financing HIV/AIDS care: A quilt with many holes", in *Capitol Hill Briefing Series on HIV/AIDS*, Oct. 2000 (http://www.kff.org/content/2000/1607/).

[2] ILO: *ILO action against HIV/AIDS: A draft framework for global and regional initiatives*, discussion paper on HIV/AIDS and the world of work (Geneva, 1999). See also ILO: *HIV/AIDS in Africa: The impact on the world of work*, study prepared for the Africa Development Forum 2000, Addis Ababa, 3-7 Dec. 2000, and *HIV/AIDS: A threat to decent work, productivity and development*, document for discussion at the Special High-Level Meeting on HIV/AIDS and the World of Work, Geneva, 8 June 2000. These reports, as well as further information on the ILO Global Programme on HIV/AIDS and the World of Work, are available on the ILO web site, at http://www.ilo.org/aids.

The transition in Central and Eastern European countries led to unprecedented unemployment, which still persists in some of these countries. In these countries and in the former USSR the responsibility for income security and certain social services has often shifted from enterprises in the context of centrally planned economies to other, often weak and inadequate, schemes, a situation which threatens to leave many workers with reduced benefits or no protection whatsoever. In South Africa, the peaceful transition from an apartheid political regime to a democratic and inclusive one has not as yet yielded decent jobs, appropriate incomes and improved economic conditions for the majority of the population.

Social security and decent work

People wish to secure a decent standard of living, within a context of security and of freedom to express their opinion and to associate. They can achieve this income security not only through productive employment, savings and accumulated assets (such as land and housing), but also through social protection mechanisms. These mechanisms function not only as a protective but also as a productive factor. Workers need income security to make long-term plans for themselves and their families. Workers' income security is also good for the economy, since it makes effective demand more predictable and provides enterprises with a more productive and flexible workforce.

The objective of most social security schemes is to provide access to health care and income security, i.e. minimum income for those in need and a reasonable replacement income for those who have contributed in proportion to their level of income. The Income Security Recommendation, 1944 (No. 67), for instance, focuses on compulsory national social insurance schemes, which in principle also cover the self-employed, and provides for social assistance. In practice, however, it has been very difficult to implement this concept in the case of workers, such as many of the self-employed, who have irregular patterns of income, for whom the concept of earnings itself is difficult to measure and who generally have different social security needs and priorities. The emergence of new contributory schemes for workers in the informal economy has highlighted this need for a wider concept. A broader social security concept could cover, for example, some housing, food security and child education benefits, in addition to the contingencies foreseen in the Social Security (Minimum Standards) Convention, 1952 (No. 102) (medical care and family benefits, as well as benefits in the event of sickness, unemployment, old age, employment injury, maternity, invalidity and death of the breadwinner).

Various authors and institutions, in particular those with experience in developing countries, have pleaded for a broader definition of social security. Some claim that — within the context of a developmental anti-poverty strategy — social security could also include policies, for example on access to productive assets, employment guarantee, minimum wages and food security. Others distinguish two aspects of social security, which are defined as the use of social means to prevent deprivation (promote living standards) and vulnerability to deprivation (protect against falling living standards). Many international organizations, including the ILO, also use the broader concept of "social protection", which covers not only social security but also non-statutory schemes; the Statistical Office of the European Communities (Eurostat) includes in its figures for social protection certain social services such as crèches and home help.

The goal and concept of decent work match this broader concept of social security. In his first Report to the International Labour Conference, the Director-General of the International Labour Office, Mr. Juan Somavia, introduced the "decent work for all" strategy, which established as the primary goal of the ILO "to promote opportunities for women and men to obtain decent and productive work, in conditions of freedom, equity, security and human dignity".[1] The decent work strategy adopts a broad perspective on work, which includes not only (paid) employment, but also work at home so as to take gender roles into consideration. Decent social protection can therefore play an important role in achieving gender equality (see Chapter IV), if all people — working men and women (remunerated or not), as well as children and the elderly — can have independent access to social protection.

One of the essential features of the decent work approach is that everybody is entitled to basic social protection. The right to social security for everyone is already laid down in article 9 of the International Covenant on Economic, Social and Cultural Rights. A decent work strategy therefore aims at universality of coverage (see also Chapter III), which has now been translated into the official goal of the Social Protection Sector: enhancing the coverage and effectiveness of social protection for all. As noted earlier, this goal is far from being achieved.

It is obvious that not all societies can afford the same level of social security. Yet it is inhuman anywhere to live and work in permanent insecurity threatening the material security and health of individuals or families. An essentially rich world can afford a minimum of security for all its inhabitants. That minimum might range from basic health services and basic food, shelter and educational rights in the poorest countries to more elaborate income security schemes in the industrialized countries. Everyone of working age has a responsibility to contribute to the social and economic progress of the community or country he or she lives in and should be given the opportunity to do so. In exchange, all have the right to a fair share of the country's or community's income and wealth.

In a globalizing world, where people are increasingly exposed to global economic risks, there is growing consciousness of the fact that a broad-based national social protection policy can provide a strong buffer against many of the negative social effects of crises. However, such a policy might need to be complemented by new international and possibly global financing mechanisms (see Chapter V), as proposed by the recent "Social Summit+5" Special Session of the United Nations General Assembly in Geneva. These proposals concern, inter alia, the possible establishment of a (voluntary) World Solidarity Fund, international cooperation in tax matters, debt relief, living up to development aid commitments and the provision of more concessional financing.

---

[1] ILO: *Decent work,* Report of the Director-General, International Labour Conference, 87th Session, Geneva, 1999, p. 3.

Some key issues

Taking into account the profound global changes affecting social security and the essential features of a decent work approach, this report will review the following key issues.

Social security, employment and development

Chapter II takes stock of the various arguments about the social and economic effects of social security. Most of the current debate seems to be focused on its alleged negative effects, but the chapter also highlights various positive effects, and then attempts to assess the conditions for the validity of the various arguments. It examines the role of unemployment insurance schemes, particularly in middle-income countries. It then discusses the potential benefits of limited employment guarantee schemes that could provide temporary employment for underemployed workers, mainly in poorer developing countries. Lastly, the chapter reviews various ways in which social security and employment policies can reinforce each other, and how these synergies depend on the socio-economic circumstances of individual countries.

Extending the personal coverage of social protection

Chapter III reviews four principal ways to extend social protection, i.e. extending statutory social insurance, promoting microinsurance, developing universal schemes and providing means-tested benefits. In the industrialized countries, statutory social security systems are well established, but determined action is necessary in various countries to prevent coverage being eroded by informalization of labour markets. In most middle-income countries, it may be possible to draw new non-covered groups into the national statutory social security system. However, in middle- and particularly in low-income countries, it may also be necessary to promote microinsurance schemes so as to cover certain groups in the informal economy that have some contributory capacity. Universal and means-tested benefits and services are alternative ways to provide social security to the population. Where national resources are not available to finance such benefits, as is often the case in low-income countries, international resources are sometimes made available, particularly in times of crisis. In general, there is a need for an integrated approach at the national level, providing linkages between various mechanisms and policies and avoiding the danger of a two-track system for those included in and those excluded from the national system.

Contributing to gender equality

Chapter IV reviews various ways in which social security can contribute to the attainment of gender equality. Most social security systems were originally structured to cater for families with a male breadwinner. As a result of changing lifestyles, expectations and family structures, a large proportion of the population does not live in such families, which has added to the demand for gender equality. Part of the challenge for social security is to respond to these changes by guaranteeing equality of treatment between men and women and, at the same time, to phase in the equalizing measures, concerning for example pensionable age and survivors' benefits. A further challenge is to use social protection, such as crèche facilities, as well as social benefits for parents and children, to attain greater gender equality and a more equal sharing of responsibilities at work and at home.

Sustainable financing for social protection

Chapter V suggests that the extension of social protection will require improved national financing as well as new forms of financing at the local and global levels. At the national level, financing could be enhanced through better collection of existing social security contributions and taxes. The "pay-as-you-go" (PAYG) form of financing would probably be most appropriate for short-term benefits, such as health insurance and maternity benefits. In the case of old-age benefits, it is shown that PAYG and advance funding are both vulnerable to demographic change. At the local level, more emphasis could be put on resources available to local governments as well as on tapping the contributory capacity of workers in the informal economy for microinsurance schemes. The financial sustainability of such schemes can be enhanced through various mechanisms, such as pooling, reinsurance and some form of affiliation with statutory social insurance schemes. At the global level, new sources might be found for financing some form of basic social protection for all, as well as measures to cope with the consequences of crises.

Expanding social dialogue

As argued in Chapter VI, the prospects of decent social protection for all can be improved by broadening the underlying social protection partnership and galvanizing the social actors. The chapter reviews the roles of the various actors in providing social protection and suggests ways in which partnerships can be formed among them to enhance the effectiveness of social security and to extend social protection through statutory social insurance, microinsurance schemes and tax-based social benefits. The chapter concludes by pointing out briefly how social dialogue could be expanded at the national and international levels.

The aim of the report

The aim of this report is to raise a number of key issues on the future of social security in a fundamentally changed global context. Its ambition is not to suggest definitive answers but to promote consensus on the assessment of the situation and on possible ways to go forward. Chapter VII gives some pointers to what the implications for the ILO could be, in terms of knowledge-based activities, standards, services and advocacy.

Human resources development and training are understood in this report to be activities of education, initial training, continuous training, and lifelong learning that develop and maintain individuals' employability and productivity over a lifetime.

Chapter II

Social security, employment and development

There is considerable controversy about the social and economic effects of social security, and most of the current debate is focused on its supposedly negative effects. Social security is said to discourage people from working and saving, to reduce international competitiveness and employment creation, and to encourage people to withdraw from the labour market prematurely. On the other hand, social security can also be seen to have a number of very positive economic effects. It can help to make people capable of earning an income and to increase their productive potential; it may help to maintain effective demand at the national level; and it may help create conditions in which a market economy can flourish, notably by encouraging workers to accept innovation and change. As noted in Chapter I, social protection and decent employment are both necessary components for a market economy to provide income security for all. Social protection is also designed to have important positive effects on society as a whole, by promoting social cohesion and a general feeling of security among its members. The first section of this chapter therefore takes stock of the various arguments and attempts to assess their validity.

Unemployment is one of the greatest social risks facing people who depend for their livelihood on the sale of their labour power. Yet unemployment benefit systems exist only in a minority of countries and many workers, including almost all the self-employed, are not covered by them. Protection against the risk of unemployment is provided not only by benefits but also by measures of employment protection (such as protection against dismissal[1]) and promotion. The second section gives a brief worldwide review of social protection against unemployment and its interaction with labour market and employment policies.

The third section sums up the main findings and highlights the need for closer linkages between policies for development, employment and decent social protection.

The social and economic impact of social security

The mechanisms by which social protection influences socio-economic development involve the behaviour of individuals, as workers and jobseekers, as savers,

---

[1] See Termination of Employment Convention, 1982 (No. 158) (Short survey), document GB.279/LILS/WP/PRS/1/3 (Geneva, ILO, 2000).

as portfolio investors and as members of civil society. They involve the decisions of firms and enterprises, and the operation of markets, including the determination of wages and prices.

In the case of the labour market, social protection has an impact on labour force participation. Benefits can encourage people to leave the labour force, for example where there is provision for early retirement. Conversely, social protection may induce people to participate in the formal economy, on account of the prospective entitlement to pensions and other benefits. Social protection can also have an impact on employment. Do benefits cause people to be slower about finding a new job when they are unemployed? Does unemployment benefit allow better worker/ employer matches? Then there is the question of the extent of productive labour input. Do sickness benefits reduce hours worked, by encouraging absence from work, or is such an effect offset by the way they help promote quick recovery and prevent the spread of infection among the workforce? Does social protection form part of a package which causes workers to be more productive? Answering these questions is not easy, as other variables have to be held constant in order to isolate the effects of social protection. It may be added that, if effects on worker productivity are considered here, this in no way disregards the fact that social protection finds its primary justification in the impact it has on workers' well-being.

In the capital market, the existence of state pensions is held by some economists to have reduced the rate of *personal savings*. This is a complex issue on which — as shown in Chapter V — empirical studies are not conclusive.

Social security expenditure, unemployment and growth

Much of the concern about social protection's economic impact centres on the effect on unemployment and on economic objectives such as productivity growth. In figure 2.1, countries are ranked by the percentage of GDP allocated to expenditure on social security transfers. Care has been taken to base the analysis on data covering a substantial period of time. This is important, since a similar analysis carried out over a shorter period might give a misleading impression, especially if it were in the 1990s, when the countries of the European Union (EU) — high social security spenders — were pursuing a restrictive macroeconomic policy at the expense of high unemployment in order to gain admission to the monetary union.

On the left of the diagram are those countries with a low level of social protection, including Australia, Japan and the United States. On the right are those countries with a relatively high level of social security expenditure, such as Belgium and the Netherlands. There is no apparent relationship between expenditure and the economic variables in question. There are countries with relatively low unemployment rates (see first panel) both on the left of the diagram, such as Japan and the United States, and on the right, such as Austria and Sweden, but the highest rates are to be found in the middle (Ireland and Spain).

Unemployment affects the level of national output, but the level of productivity also needs to be taken into account. Economies differ in GDP per hour worked in

Figure 2.1. Selected economic indicators for OECD countries ranked by the percentage of GDP devoted to social security expenditure (lowest on left, highest on right)

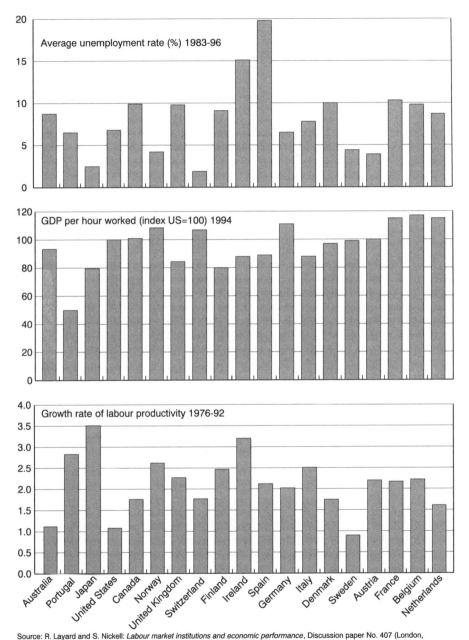

Source: R. Layard and S. Nickell: *Labour market institutions and economic performance*, Discussion paper No. 407 (London, Centre for Economic Performance, 1998), cited in ILO: *World Labour Report 2000: Income security and social protection in a changing world* (Geneva, 2000), p. 62.

ways that are not widely known. The productivity estimates in the second panel of figure 2.1 show that GDP per hour worked in the United States is twice that in Portugal but lower than that in a number of European countries. The countries with the highest social security expenditure have productivity per hour which at least matches that in the United States (this productivity measure takes no account of the contribution of factors other than labour).

Current levels of productivity are a reflection of past differences in growth rates. The third panel of figure 2.1 shows the growth performance of different economies over the period since the first oil shock. Labour productivity, measured as GDP per hour worked, grew strongly in Japan, but also in Ireland, Italy and other European countries. Growth in this period was low in Sweden,[2] but the same was true of the United States.

Lastly, it should be stressed that the indices of performance considered are those conventional in economic analysis, but their limitations are well known. They deal with marketed output, but there are other important dimensions of activities (non-marketed output, quality of working life, effects on the environment) which contribute to the ultimate goal of improving human welfare. In particular, security can be viewed as a good that citizens demand, but which the market, in various cases, is not well equipped to provide efficiently, because of economies of scale, adverse selection and transaction cost problems. This would help to explain the relative stability of social security systems despite their allegedly having been in "crisis" for the last 30 years.

Productivity and social stability

It has been suggested by various commentators that social security contributes to economic growth by raising labour productivity and enhancing social stability. Various types of social security are particularly relevant to labour productivity:

● Health-care systems help to maintain workers in good health and to cure those who become sick. Poor health is a major cause of low productivity in many developing countries where workers do not have access to adequate health care. Not only does it limit their ability to cope with the physical demands of their jobs, but it also leads to sickness absence and can seriously undermine efficiency even among workers who do not absent themselves from work. Care for workers' family members helps to ensure the good health of the future labour force.

● Pension systems ease the departure of older workers from the labour force, thereby helping to avoid the problem of workers remaining in employment when their productivity has fallen to a low level.

● Cash sickness benefit contributes to the recovery of sick workers by removing the financial pressure to carry on working when ill. It also helps to maintain the productivity of other workers by countering the spread of infection.

---

[2] The low productivity growth rate in Sweden, and perhaps in certain other OECD countries as well, during this period is thought to result not from low productivity growth in the old "core" sectors, but rather from the huge expansion of the service sector, especially the labour-intensive health and caring professions.

- Maternity insurance is of particular importance for the reproduction of a healthy workforce, as well as for the maintenance of the health of working mothers.

- Work injury schemes — the oldest and most widespread form of social security — are playing an increasingly important role in preventing work-related accidents and sickness and in rehabilitating workers who fall victim to these. Such activities are of considerable relevance to productivity, given the enormous numbers of days off work attributable to avoidable health risks.

- Unemployment benefit provides unemployed workers with the breathing space they need in order to find suitable work which makes full use of their talents and potential; the associated employment and training services are also highly relevant in this respect.

- Child benefits (and other cash benefits provided when the breadwinner is unable to work) help to ensure that families with children have enough income to provide proper nutrition and a healthy living environment for their children. In developing countries, child benefits can also be a powerful instrument to combat child labour and promote school attendance. Children can thus receive an education that will permit them in the long run to attain much higher levels of productivity and income.

More indirect effects on productivity may also be important. The existence of a good unemployment insurance system creates a feeling of security among the workforce which can greatly facilitate structural change and technological innovations that workers might otherwise perceive as a great threat to their livelihoods. The link between these issues was graphically illustrated in the Republic of Korea by the Tripartite Accord of 1998 under which workers' organizations accepted greater labour market flexibility, including lay-offs, in exchange for better social protection.

Social security helps create a more positive attitude not just to structural and technological change, but also to the challenges of globalization and to its potential benefits in terms of greater efficiency and higher productivity. Countries with relatively open national economies (a high ratio of trade to GDP) and high exposure to external risks (high variability in the relative prices of imports and exports) have been observed to provide high levels of social security. It appears that societies which expose themselves to more external risk demand a higher degree of social protection. Globalization and social security thus tend to be mutually reinforcing.

Social security can be an important factor in the maintenance of effective demand and of business confidence. This effect is most obvious in the case of unemployment benefits, which help to maintain the purchasing power of workers who have lost their jobs. However, other social security benefits also act as an economic buffer during a recession or crisis. Without them, the multiplier effects of the first round of job losses could be followed by second and third rounds that could cut deep into the social fabric of the community, as well as leaving much of the economy working well below capacity. Social security thus helps to prevent production from falling too far and to keep companies in business, with their workforce intact, ready to participate in the upswing when it comes.

Table 2.1.   Income tax plus employee and employer social security contributions (as percentage of labour costs), 1998[1]

Country[2]	Income tax	Social security contributions		Total[4]	Labour costs[5]
		Employee	Employer[3]		
Belgium	22	10	26	57	40 995
Germany	17	17	17	52	35 863
Switzerland	9	10	10	30	32 535
Italy	14	7	26	47	32 351
Netherlands	6	23	14	44	32 271
Denmark	34	10	1	44	32 214
Canada	20	5	6	32	32 211
Norway	19	7	11	37	31 638
United States	17	7	7	31	31 300
Luxembourg	10	11	12	34	31 102
Austria	8	14	24	46	29 823
Sweden	21	5	25	51	29 768
Australia	24	2	0	25	29 590
Finland	22	6	21	49	29 334
United Kingdom	15	8	9	32	29 277
France	10	9	28	48	28 198
Japan	6	7	7	20	27 664
Ireland	18	5	11	33	24 667
Spain	11	5	24	39	24 454
New Zealand	20	0	0	20	24 332
Korea, Rep. of	1	4	9	15	22 962
Iceland	20	0	4	25	22 545
Greece	2	12	22	36	17 880
Turkey	21	8	11	40	15 825
Czech Republic	8	9	26	43	15 781
Portugal	6	9	19	34	13 903
Poland	11	0	33	43	12 696
Hungary	12	8	32	52	9 916
Mexico	0	2	20	22	8 662

[1] Single individual at the income level of the average production worker.   [2] Countries ranked by decreasing labour costs.   [3] Employer social security contributions include reported payroll taxes.   [4] Owing to rounding total may differ by one percentage point from aggregate of columns for income tax and social security contributions.   [5] Dollars with equal purchasing power. Labour costs include gross wages plus employers' compulsory social security contributions.

Source: OECD: *Taxing wages in OECD countries 1998/1999: Taxes on wages and salaries, social security contributions for employees and their employers, child benefits — 1999 edition* (Paris, 2000), bilingual edition.

Employer contributions and international competitiveness

Widespread concern has been expressed in business and political circles that high employer contributions to social security make national economies less competitive, a claim frequently heard in discussions of globalization. Most economists, however, have taken the view that in the long run, through the normal working of market forces, these costs will be borne by workers in the form of lower wages (lower, that is, than they would receive in an identical economy without any payroll tax or employer social security contributions). As a result, employer contributions probably do not affect total labour costs in the long term. This appears to be borne out by OECD figures given in table 2.1, which ranks OECD countries according to their labour costs (defined as gross wages plus employer social security contributions). The ten countries with the highest labour costs include only two with high employer contributions (of 20 per cent or more). Of the next ten countries, five have high employer contributions. The proportion of countries with a high level of employer contributions is in fact greatest (five out of nine) in the countries with the *lowest* labour costs.

In the short term, however, an *increase* in employer contributions may well be reflected in higher labour costs. And this effect could last for quite some time, particularly if labour and product markets are imperfect and if the increase takes place during a period of low growth and low inflation, when employers typically have less room for manoeuvre in wage negotiations. This means that it is very important to avoid large increases in contributions: several small increases phased over a number of years will be very much easier for the economy to absorb than a single large increase.

Empirical evidence suggests that social security contributions do not have any long-run impact on unemployment.[3] This helps to explain why Denmark, the only country in Europe with virtually no employer contributions, has over the years had unemployment on a par with the European average and appears to derive no special employment advantage from its lack of such contributions. Governments often believe that a reduction in social security contributions will reduce labour costs. The experience of Chile before and after its social security pension reform has been investigated in order to establish the impact of the sharp reduction in contributions. The average payroll tax rate in the sample of manufacturing firms covered by the research fell from 30 per cent to 5 per cent over the period between 1979 and 1985. Strong evidence is found that the reduction was fully offset by higher wages, leaving labour costs unreduced.[4]

All this should not be taken to suggest that there is no limit to the level of social security contributions. In any democratic society the political preferences of the majority most certainly impose a limit. Depending on what people perceive as desirable and fair, that limit is much lower in some countries than others. Moreover, if the level of contributions rises very high, this creates strong incentives for non-compliance, which if not controlled will seriously undermine the system.

---

[3] See *World Labour Report 2000,* op. cit., p. 68; and S.J. Nickell: "Unemployment and labor market rigidities: Europe versus North America", in *Journal of Economic Perspectives* (Minneapolis, Minnesota), Vol. 11, No. 3, 1997, pp. 55-74.

[4] Jonathan Gruber: *The incidence of payroll taxation: Evidence from Chile,* NBER Working Paper No. W5053 (Cambridge, Mass., National Bureau of Economic Research, 1995).

Unemployment benefits, unemployment and employment

Much research has been carried out to investigate the hypothesis that the average duration of unemployment benefit receipt is positively related both to the level of unemployment benefits (the replacement ratio) and to the maximum duration of benefit. Various studies have confirmed that significant relationships exist, but that their effects are modest.[5]

An important question left unanswered by many of these studies is what happens to people once they cease to receive unemployment benefit. It cannot simply be assumed that they find regular employment. Recent work has investigated this issue. In Bulgaria those without unemployment benefit are more likely to leave registered unemployment, but it is to inactivity rather than to employment. In Slovakia, changes in eligibility periods result in people leaving unemployment not so much to take up regular jobs as for "other reasons". People in Sweden not receiving unemployment benefit were found to be much more likely to leave the labour market or to take up places in active labour market programmes.[6] In other countries those who cease to receive unemployment benefit often move into informal or even criminal activities, resulting in massive tax evasion and other costs to society. Since lack of benefit entitlement may simply be causing people to quit the labour force, it may be more important to examine the relationship between unemployment benefit and employment: after all the real concern is that people may be drawing unemployment benefit when they could be employed instead. A recent study[7] concluded, on the basis of cross-country evidence, that there is in fact no connection between unemployment benefits and total employment. This study also found that high unemployment was associated with the absence of complementary active labour market policies.

Early retirement

In recent years there has been great concern about the adverse effects which early retirement provisions may have upon employment as well as upon pension costs. These had been introduced during periods of high unemployment, particularly among older workers, in the hope of creating more job openings for younger workers. As unemployment has fallen, early retirement provisions in numerous social security systems have been tightened or even abolished. However, there has been little or no change in retirement behaviour. This paradox is explained by a number of factors:

- the proportion of older workers receiving unemployment benefits remains relatively high and includes many who have, for all intents and purposes, retired;

---

[5] See, for example, Anthony B. Atkinson and John Micklewright: "Unemployment compensation and labor market transitions: A critical review", in *Journal of Economic Literature* (Nashville, Tennessee), Vol. 29, No. 4, 1991, pp. 1679-1727.

[6] *World Labour Report 2000,* op. cit., p. 154.

[7] Nickell, op. cit.

- employer pension schemes often contain strong incentives to retire early;
- even workers without unemployment benefits or private pension entitlements are quitting the labour force before standard pensionable age, many of them manual workers for whom demand is low and who are often in poor health.

Unemployment benefits and employment promotion

It was estimated that at the end of 1998 some 1 billion workers — or one-third of the world's labour force — were either unemployed or underemployed. The actual number of unemployed people — that is, seeking or available for work but unable to find it — was about 150 million. In addition, 25 to 30 per cent of the world's workers were underemployed, that is, either working substantially less than full time, but wishing to work longer, or earning less than a living wage. It is striking to see not only how many workers are affected in absolute terms, but also how rapidly the situation can change. For example, as a result of the Asian financial crisis, one in 20 workers in the Republic of Korea lost their jobs during the nine months from November 1997 to July 1998 and open unemployment jumped from 2.3 to 8 per cent between the end of 1997 and the beginning of 1999.

Unemployment benefit systems protect employees in the industrialized countries and in a number of middle-income developing countries. In most developing countries no unemployment benefits exist as such, but some of the unemployed may be able to get a limited amount of paid work in labour-intensive programmes. Of the world's unemployed, probably not more than a quarter are entitled to unemployment benefit.

Relevant international labour standards

The most recently adopted instruments are the Employment Promotion and Protection against Unemployment Convention, 1988 (No. 168), and Recommendation (No. 176). The contingencies covered by the Convention include full unemployment "defined as the loss of earnings due to inability to obtain suitable employment [...] in the case of a person capable of working, available for work and actually seeking work". Member States shall in addition endeavour to extend the protection of the Convention to two other contingencies:

- loss of earnings due to partial unemployment (short-time working); and
- suspension or reduction of earnings due to a temporary suspension of work; as well as to part-time workers who are actually seeking full-time work.

Persons protected under the Convention "shall comprise prescribed classes of employees, constituting not less than 85 per cent of all employees". Compared with previous Conventions dealing with unemployment benefit (the Unemployment Provision Convention, 1934 (No. 44), and the Social Security (Minimum Standards) Convention, 1952 (No. 102), Part IV), an innovative feature of Convention No. 168 is that it requires the payment of "social benefits" to at least three of the following ten categories of new applicants for employment: young persons who have completed their vocational training; young people who have completed their studies; young people who have completed their compulsory military service; people seeking work after a period devoted to bringing up a child or caring for someone who is sick, disabled or elderly; people whose spouse had died, when they are not entitled to a survivor's benefit; divorced or separated persons; released prisoners; adults, including disabled persons, who have completed a period of training; migrant workers returning to their home country (except in so far as they have acquired rights under the legislation of the country where they last worked); and previously self-employed persons.

The benefits under the Convention are not less than 50 per cent of previous earnings in earnings-related systems, while in other types of system they must be fixed at not less than 50 per cent of the minimum wage or of the wage of an ordinary labourer, or at a level that provides the minimum essential for basic living expenses, whichever of the three is the highest.

Industrialized countries

Within the industrialized countries there is substantial variation in unemployment benefit systems. One group of countries is characterized by the high level and long duration of their unemployment insurance benefits, by extensive coverage and by the existence of a fall-back benefit system of unemployment assistance for workers who have exhausted their insurance entitlements. These countries include Austria, Belgium, Denmark, Finland, France, Germany, Iceland, Luxembourg, Netherlands, Norway, Portugal, Spain, Sweden and Switzerland. They generally have not only good benefits, but also a high level of employment protection.

A second group of countries, including Australia, Canada, Japan, New Zealand, the United Kingdom and the United States, have systems which provide lower benefits. According to the OECD employment protection ranking, the legal arrangements in these countries apparently provide relatively little statutory employment protection.[8]

The countries of Central and Eastern Europe introduced unemployment benefit systems about the end of the 1980s which were initially rather generous, but have since been reduced, particularly in terms of benefit duration. Benefit levels as a percentage of wages are similar to those in Western Europe, but a much lower proportion of the unemployed receive benefits in these countries — for example, about one-third of the registered unemployed in Poland.

Unemployment benefit schemes have become more and more inadequate as individual employment patterns have become increasingly uncertain. These schemes therefore have to be flexible enough to cover new uncertainties and changes facing workers and have to form part of larger strategies for employment and economic development.

Employment protection policies in the industrialized countries have been concerned in particular with the high rates of unemployment affecting unskilled workers. One approach has stressed the need for better education and training to ensure that workers have the skills that are in demand in a high-wage, high-productivity

---

[8] *World Labour Report 2000,* op. cit., p. 149.

economy. Another approach has been to use social protection to subsidize unskilled labour, either through the payment of income-tested benefits to the working poor or through the (partial or total) exemption of their employers from paying social insurance contributions on their behalf (with the cost being borne by the State).

Middle-income developing countries

Unemployment benefit systems are at best in their formative stages in the middle-income developing countries: the duration and level of benefits are generally low and coverage is much more limited than in the industrialized countries. On the other hand, formal-sector employees are covered by various forms of employment protection legislation in a number of middle-income developing countries, including some that do not have any unemployment benefits. The legislation typically includes severance pay, which can help to tide redundant workers over a period of unemployment. However, these are lump-sum payments, the size of which depends on the length of previous service, not on the occurrence or duration of unemployment. Severance payments have traditionally been an employer's liability. However, in some Latin American countries in the 1990s they were replaced by mandatory severance savings schemes. This change has meant that the funds are invested in the capital market rather than retained within the firm. While this introduces uncertainty as to the amount of benefit that workers will receive, it guards against the risk that an insolvent employer may fail to provide severance pay.

Most unemployment benefit schemes in the developing countries, as in the industrialized world, are financed by employer and worker contributions, but in certain Latin American countries such as Brazil and Chile they are financed from tax revenue. Where unemployment benefits exist, the proportion of the total unemployed receiving them tends to be low. The replacement rate (benefits as a proportion of previous wages) varies between 40 and 80 per cent in Latin America and the Caribbean and is 45 per cent in South Africa. Benefit duration tends to be fairly limited and is often related to the length of time that the worker has been insured. In China the locally set rates of unemployment benefit are generally low. Hong Kong, China, provides benefits on a means-tested basis as part of its social assistance system to registered unemployed persons with at least one year's residence. The Republic of Korea has expanded its unemployment insurance system to cover about half of all employees, but those in small enterprises — who are often the most vulnerable — are still excluded.

The recent Asian financial crisis has made it clear that unemployment insurance schemes could have played a substantial role in coping with the unacceptable levels of hardship caused by rapidly escalating unemployment. They would also have helped to limit the collapse of consumer demand and business confidence which made the crisis much more acute than it would otherwise have been. As was shown in an ILO feasibility study carried out for the Government of Thailand, the contribution rate necessary to finance a modest unemployment insurance scheme would in the long run be less than 1 per cent of earnings.

Implementing unemployment insurance in the context of a developing country represents a considerable challenge. Employment services, where they exist, tend to be rudimentary and have to be upgraded in order to provide meaningful help to unemployed workers to find other work, as well as to monitor whether they are in fact willing and available to take up employment. A second problem is that much employment in these countries is not effectively covered by social security — either because it is excluded from the legislation, which may apply only to workers in firms above a certain size, or because employers and workers do not comply with the legislation.

The reality for most workers in developing countries, even countries in the middle-income category, is that their jobs are not covered, because they are self-employed or because they are employed in the informal economy or in small enterprises. To help protect them in the event of unemployment, other measures are needed, such as the opportunity to obtain employment in labour-intensive public works. It is important to note that when people lose their jobs and have no access to benefits, they must usually resort to informal-sector activity in order to survive: they may therefore be more accurately described as underemployed than unemployed.

Other developing countries

In so far as other developing countries have taken measures to provide some protection for the unemployed and underemployed, these have tended to take the form of employment-intensive programmes. These are undertaken mainly during the lean season, when small farmers and landless workers are not engaged in agricultural activities and have no alternative sources of employment. In an urban setting they can also be implemented during periods of recession or economic crisis. These programmes can both generate employment and reduce poverty by using labour-based techniques for mainstream investment programmes and by directing investments increasingly towards the productive and social needs of the low-income groups in the population. Some programmes of this type operate on a large scale. For example, the Jawahar Rozgar Yojana (JRY) programme in India by the mid-1990s covered over one-third of the country's underdeveloped districts and provided some 20 days' work a year to each participant. Similar programmes operate on a smaller scale in countries such as Bolivia, Botswana, Chile, Honduras, Kenya, the United Republic of Tanzania and (recently) South Africa, and the umbrella organization AFRICATIP groups together some 18 executing agencies in French- and Portuguese-speaking African countries which organize public works for implementation by small local contractors, with a view to boosting employment.

A salient feature of employment-intensive programmes is that they "self-select" the people who participate in them. Since they pay only the going agricultural wage in the region (or the minimum wage if this is set realistically), only low-income workers are attracted to them. This avoids the cumbersome and costly administrative arrangements that would be necessary if assistance were to be provided to such people on a means-tested basis. The programmes have the advantage that they are open both to wage earners and to people who normally work on their own account (whose needs may in some cases be just as great). Employment under a labour-intensive programme can be organized so that workers can obtain an employment guarantee for a certain number of days per year, which thus provides a kind of income security. The guarantee is most extensive where employment is provided on demand.

Conclusions: Linking social security with employment and development policies

This chapter has shown that there is a complex relationship between social security, employment and development. At the macro level, at least for the industrialized countries, there does not seem to be a clear relationship between social security expenditure, productivity and unemployment. However, at the sectoral and enterprise levels there is good reason to believe that there is a positive relation between productivity and social security. This is particularly true for health insurance, which boosts workers' productivity, and for child benefits when they are linked to school attendance. The evidence in this chapter also shows that employer contributions do not seem to have a long-term impact on labour costs and international competitiveness, since the burden of all social security contributions is in the end absorbed by workers in the form of lower wages. Finally, there is evidence — for some industrialized countries — that the level and duration of unemployment benefits exert a modest adverse effect on unemployment, but that this effect can be reduced through better design of benefits and supporting labour market policies.

Worldwide, probably not more than one-quarter of the 150 million unemployed people are covered by unemployment benefits, and they are mainly concentrated in the industrialized countries. But for those who work in the rural or urban informal sectors in the developing countries hardly any unemployment protection exists. In the industrialized countries, the most important issue is probably to extend the personal coverage of unemployment insurance schemes — in coordination with labour market policies. In most middle-income developing countries, unemployment insurance can — at a relatively modest cost — play a substantial role in coping with the unacceptable levels of hardship caused by rapidly escalating unemployment. However, the majority of workers outside the formal economy could only be protected against unemployment through macroeconomic policies, such as demand-stimulating policies, and direct employment promotion measures, such as enterprise development, training and employment-intensive programmes.

Social security policies are part of — and interact with — a wide range of social policies, such as investments in basic social services, protective labour legislation and the enforcement of basic rights. They are also intimately related to employment policies, because most social insurance schemes are financed out of labour incomes and protect against risks related to employment capacity, such as unemployment, sickness, disability and old age. Favourable social security and employment outcomes are strongly influenced by economic development, and all of them contribute to the process of socio-economic development.

As noted in Chapter I, social security is increasingly seen as an integral part of the development process. It is therefore necessary to look for synergies between policies for social protection, employment and development. These synergies exist in various areas of social policy, such as health, education, housing and social welfare, but also in areas of economic policy, such as macroeconomic and sectoral policies (for instance, small-scale enterprise development). However, the potential synergies are probably strongest with regard to employment and labour market policies.

This chapter has turned the spotlight on the economy, in recognition of the very real economic effects which social security may have. There is of course the more fundamental question: What is the purpose of economic activity? The concepts of decent work and people-centred development, embracing social security, must then take centre stage.

Chapter III

Extending the personal coverage of social protection

The right to social security

International instruments adopted by the ILO and the United Nations affirm that every human being has the right to social security. In the Declaration of Philadelphia (1944) the International Labour Conference recognized the ILO's obligation as regards "the extension of social security measures to provide a basic income to all in need of such protection and comprehensive medical care". The ILO's Income Security Recommendation, 1944 (No. 67), provides that "social insurance should afford protection, in the contingencies to which they are exposed, to all employed and self-employed persons, together with their dependants" (Paragraph 17). The Universal Declaration of Human Rights, 1948, states that "everyone, as a member of society, has the right to social security [...]" (article 22), and refers specifically to the right to medical care and necessary social services, to security in the event of sickness, disability, widowhood, old age and unemployment, and to special care and assistance for motherhood and childhood (article 25). The International Covenant on Economic, Social and Cultural Rights, 1966, recognizes "the right of everyone to social security, including social insurance" (article 9).

It goes without saying that the practical implementation of this right requires a major undertaking by the State and the community. The ILO's social security Conventions recognize that in practice the ideal may be difficult to attain. For example, the Social Security (Minimum Standards) Convention, 1952 (No. 102) requires in the case of sickness and old-age benefits, for instance, that persons covered shall comprise:

- prescribed classes of employees, constituting not less than 50 per cent of all employees; *or*
- prescribed classes of the economically active population, constituting not less than 20 per cent of all residents; *or*
- all residents whose means during the contingency do not exceed prescribed limits.

These alternatives are intended to facilitate ratification of the Convention by countries, whatever type of social security system they may have. Later Conventions such as the Invalidity, Old-Age and Survivors' Benefits Convention, 1967 (No. 128), contain more exacting standards, but provide a similar choice.

The Plantations Convention, 1958 (No. 110), applies to workers hired by agricultural undertakings in the tropical or subtropical regions of the world. In terms of social security its standards are less exacting than those of Convention No. 102. It requires that plantation workers be covered by workers' compensation and maternity protection, including a minimum of 12 weeks' paid leave. The Convention also contains provisions relating to medical care.

During the 1990s new ILO instruments have sought to promote social security coverage for persons outside regular wage employment. Thus, the Home Work Convention, 1996 (No. 177), provides that national policy on home work shall promote, as far as possible, equality of treatment between homeworkers and other wage earners in areas including statutory social security protection and maternity protection. The accompanying Recommendation (No. 184) proposes that social protection can be achieved through the extension and adaptation of existing social security schemes and/or through the development of special schemes or funds. The Job Creation in Small and Medium-Sized Enterprises Recommendation, 1998 (No. 189), recommends that labour and social legislation be reviewed inter alia to determine whether social protection extends to workers in these enterprises, whether there are adequate provisions to ensure compliance with social security regulations covering the standard contingencies and whether there is a need for supplementary social protection measures for workers in these categories. The Part-Time Work Convention, 1994 (No. 175), states that social security schemes shall be adapted so that part-time workers enjoy conditions equivalent to those of comparable full-time workers.

The problem of non-coverage

A very large proportion of the population in most regions of the world still does not enjoy any social protection or is covered only very partially. This is the case for the vast majority of people in developing countries, and even in some of the richest industrialized countries there are large and growing gaps in social protection.

Informal economy workers are not covered by social security for a variety of reasons. One is the extreme difficulty of collecting contributions from them and, as the case may be, from their employers. Another problem is that many of these workers are unable to contribute a relatively high percentage of their incomes to financing social security benefits and unwilling to do so when these benefits do not meet their priority needs. Their most immediate priorities tend to include health care, in particular where structural adjustment measures have reduced access to free services. They feel less need for pensions, for example, as for many of them old age appears very remote and the idea of retirement perhaps unreal. Unfamiliarity with social security schemes and distrust of the way they are managed add to their reluctance to contribute.

The problem of low coverage is of course not new, especially in countries where large numbers of people work in subsistence agriculture. However, in recent years, prospects of resolving or at least mitigating it have taken a dramatic turn for the worse, as an increasing proportion of the urban labour force is working in the informal economy, inter alia as a result of structural adjustment.

In Latin America and many other parts of the developing world in recent years most of the increase in the urban labour force has taken place in the informal economy. In most countries of Africa, a growing proportion of the urban labour force is active in the informal economy, reflecting the (at best) sluggish growth of wage employment, the massive migration to the cities and the need for workers to supplement falling wages with earnings from the informal economy. For example, in the case of Kenya, informal employment accounted for almost two-thirds of total urban employment in 1996, compared with just 10 per cent in 1972.[1] Several developing countries of Asia have expanded wage employment substantially but the informal economy remains very important almost everywhere. In India, for example, if agriculture is included, more than 90 per cent of workers are to be found in the informal economy.

It should be noted that the informal economy is not a "sector" as such. It is in fact a phenomenon to be found in almost all sectors. And it includes workers of all different categories: employees, self-employed, homeworkers, unpaid family workers, etc. Informalization is not restricted to small-scale enterprises; in many countries it includes unregulated wage labour throughout the economy: in Argentina and Brazil, for example, approximately 40 per cent of urban wage earners are in informal employment.

In many countries a higher proportion of women work in the informal economy, to some extent because there they can more easily combine work with their heavier burden of family responsibilities, and partly for other reasons related, for example, to discrimination encountered in the formal economy. ILO statistics show that in two-thirds of the countries for which separate figures are available, the informal economy accounts for a higher share of total female urban employment than is the case for men.[2] There is a widespread tendency for women to remain trapped in the informal economy for much of their working lives, whereas for men — in the industrialized countries at any rate — it is less likely to be permanent. For long-term income security (in old age for instance), this difference has especially important implications, as women tend to live longer than men.

Informal economy workers have little or no security of employment or income. Their earnings tend to be very low and to fluctuate more than those of other workers. A brief period of incapacity can leave the worker and her or his family without enough income to live on. The sickness of a family member can result in costs which destroy the delicate balance of the household budget. Work in the informal economy is often intrinsically hazardous and the fact that it takes place in an unregulated environment makes it still more so. Women face additional disadvantages due to discrimination related to their reproductive role, such as dismissal when pregnant, or upon marriage. Women in the informal economy do not benefit from safeguards and

---

[1] ILO: *Kenya: Meeting the employment challenges of the 21st century* (Addis Ababa, East Africa Multidisciplinary Advisory Team, 1999).

[2] *World Labour Report 2000,* op. cit., statistical annex, table 7.

benefits related to child-rearing that in principle apply to women in formal wage employment (such as family allowances, paid maternity leave, nursing breaks or assistance with the cost of childcare).

It is now widely recognized that there is a pressing need to find effective ways to extend social protection. The recent past has seen a stagnation in the proportion of the labour force covered. Given current economic trends, failure to take action is very likely to lead to a reduction in the rate of coverage or even in the absolute numbers of workers protected, as has occurred in parts of sub-Saharan Africa.

Policies to achieve the extension of coverage

Outside the industrialized world, policy-makers have found few remedies for the lack of social protection. This may be because existing social protection policies are inappropriate. It may be because insufficient efforts have been made to implement these policies. Or it may be because the lack of social protection is related to much wider economic, social and political problems. If policy-makers define the problem too narrowly, their chances of finding feasible solutions may be greatly reduced. It is therefore necessary to give due consideration to the wider context in which social security systems have to operate.

The economic, social and political context

The first point to consider is the nature of a country's governance. Among market economies, experience shows that, with few exceptions, there tends to be a correlation between the level of democracy and the adequacy of social protection. For the most vulnerable members of the population to have their needs for health care and basic income security met, it is vital that they should at least be able to make their voices heard. In the long run a democracy which does not ensure adequate social protection is unlikely to survive.

The second issue which must be considered is the macroeconomic situation and the state of the labour market. The scope of social protection is likely to extend naturally (the means by which it may do so are considered below) if and only if the labour market is strong. So long as demand for labour remains weak, few people will obtain decent jobs and most will depend on ill-paid and unprotected work in the informal economy. Conversely, if the demand for labour increases, more workers may look forward to better-paid and generally better-protected employment in the formal economy. However, the informal economy — in its many manifestations — is hardly likely to disappear either naturally or quickly, and it is of the greatest importance that governments work towards social protection policies, which must be both innovative and imaginative, that will promote improved conditions for such workers.

A third point is that excessive demands should not be placed on social security systems. They are no substitute for adequate macroeconomic, regional education and housing policies and they cannot be expected to achieve a fair distribution of income on their own. Many social security systems redistribute from the rich to the poor, but this is not their main objective. The prime objective is to provide security for people when they are sick, disabled, unemployed, retired, etc. Schemes which represent reasonable value for money for all the insured have the best chance in practice of achieving high compliance rates, that is, of ensuring that legislation providing for wide coverage is actually implemented. Social security is just part — albeit an important part — of the broader package of measures necessary to reduce poverty and improve income distribution.

Finally, public confidence in social security systems is crucial if they are to attain and maintain wide coverage. This requires not only efficient administration and high standards of financial probity, but also a strong degree of commitment by the government itself to ensure the long-run health of the system. Where this confidence is lacking, people will always find ways to avoid contributing, even though their need for social protection may be very high.

Strategies for extending social protection

There are essentially four ways to extend social protection:
- extending social insurance schemes;
- encouraging microinsurance;
- introducing universal benefits or services financed from general state revenues;
- establishing or extending means-tested benefits or services (social assistance), also financed from general state revenues.

None of these approaches should be excluded a priori. The appropriate mix of different mechanisms will depend on the national context and on the national strategy adopted. Careful thought has to be given to their respective roles and to the linkages between them. Achieving a better understanding of these is essential if progress is to be made. There is a need for research, experimentation and innovation. No doubt, in this process, distinctions will be drawn between groups of countries, depending on their level of economic and social development. Within the developing countries, there are those in the middle-income category, some of which already have well-developed social security institutions. These countries, and indeed the industrialized countries where coverage is incomplete, may aim at extending compulsory coverage to all or most of the population, using the existing social insurance schemes or modifying them to suit the needs of the new categories of the population to be covered. Secondly, there is the large group of low-income countries where, if any real increase in coverage is to be achieved, it will almost certainly have to be by some of the other means mentioned above.

Extending social insurance schemes

Whenever social insurance schemes have been made compulsory for a limited section of the labour force in the formal economy, legislators have usually envisaged extending their coverage at a later stage. The initial restriction of coverage has almost invariably been justified by invoking practical constraints: for example, the administrative infrastructure did not exist which would permit the collection of contributions from workers in small firms or from the self-employed, or health-care facilities did not exist in rural areas, so workers there could not be required to contribute. These reasons were and, in many cases, remain perfectly valid. However, the question that should always be asked is what is being done to remove these constraints.

Unfortunately, the answer in many cases is that very little has been or is being done, and this for a variety of reasons:

- a lack of effective political pressure from those who are not protected and limited awareness of the benefits that social protection can bring;

- a lack of effective and efficient social partnership within certain countries and at the international level;

- the unwillingness or inability of governments to assume new and potentially costly commitments; and

- institutional inertia.

The first and, to some extent, the second reasons reflect the relatively low level of organization among people who are unprotected. The third reason has to do with the fact that subsidies, which governments sometimes provide for the minority of the population covered by the existing system, would become very much more expensive if protection were significantly extended. As for the fourth, the institutions which prepare proposals to extend coverage are often those responsible for administering the existing system and often have to do so in difficult conditions; they may have little incentive to propose extensions of coverage where these would make it still harder for them to discharge their existing responsibilities.

Removing constraints on freedom of association and strengthening democratic institutions would help address the first problem and measures to foster collective bargaining and tripartite institutions would be relevant to the second. The adverse implications for the state budget of extending social insurance coverage could be attenuated by a reduction or reorientation or, if necessary, the elimination of state subsidies — particularly where they benefit only a minority and could not conceivably be extended to the majority of the workforce. As for institutional inertia, this may be at least partially remedied by government action, for example to release the social security institution from civil service rules when these impose unrealistic limits on staffing and on pay levels, and to give it clear instructions to formulate, within a certain time frame, legislative proposals to extend coverage.

Most commonly, compulsory coverage is extended in stages by bringing into the scheme successively smaller enterprises. Each extension naturally expands the number of insured workers, but disproportionately increases the number of enterprises with which the social security system must deal. The smaller enterprises may present additional problems, given their rudimentary accounts and arrangements for paying workers and their stronger tendency to non-compliance. Many less developed social security systems understandably hesitate to try covering all employees, including those in the smallest enterprises. However, experience in numerous countries has now shown that it is feasible. Indeed, it can be advantageous to abandon any threshold and so remove an incentive for employers to report artificially low numbers of workers. Many enterprises usually claim to be just below the threshold, and it is very difficult in practice to prove otherwise. Besides, a rule which encourages enterprises to remain small can seriously hamper their development and constrain productivity growth. The most compelling reason for covering even the smallest enterprises is that it is their workers who tend to be the lowest paid and to have least job security — they need social security even more than other employees.

Attempts to extend existing social insurance schemes to cover the self-employed have met with mixed success. Few join these schemes on a voluntary basis, as they are unwilling — and indeed frequently unable — to pay the combined worker and employer contribution. Only in some cases do people not subject to compulsory coverage have a strong incentive to contribute voluntarily, for example in order to preserve their pension entitlements or to complete the minimum period required to qualify for a pension. As for compulsory coverage of the self-employed, this is difficult to achieve, given the problems involved in identifying who the self-employed are and what they earn. Some special schemes for self-employed workers tend to have more success, particularly if the government is willing to subsidize them. Specially adapted social insurance schemes can take account of the lower contributory capacity of most self-employed workers by providing a more limited benefit package than the employees' scheme. Lower contributions and concentration on benefits which are of greatest interest to the self-employed (recent ILO work in several developing countries suggests that these include not only health care, but also survivors' and invalidity insurance) make it easier to achieve compliance.

Most of the financial support currently given (via tax concessions) to voluntary coverage tends to go to *supplementary* private pension and health insurance schemes and thus to favour the higher-income groups. It is important to quantify the support that the State gives to such schemes. Such data will inform the public debate on social protection and help to define priorities in the use of public resources, so that in future state support for voluntary coverage could be much better targeted than it is now.

Recent examples of successful extensions of compulsory coverage

In 1995 Namibia launched a new scheme covering maternity, sickness and death (funeral) benefits. By 1999 an estimated 80 per cent of formal sector workers were covered and the scheme enjoyed wide popularity. The scheme provides three months of maternity benefit at 80 per cent of covered wages, and up to two years of sickness benefit at 60 per cent of wages for six months and 50 per cent thereafter.[3] The success of the scheme is attributed to its efficient administration, its low contributions and the absence of organized financial interests opposing it.

---

[3] Elaine Fultz and Bodhi Pieris: *Social security schemes in southern Africa: An overview and proposals for future development*, ILO SAMAT Discussion Paper No. 11, Dec. 1999, p. 28.

Following Bill Clinton's first election as President of the United States, one of his nominees for a senior administration appointment was asked during her confirmation hearing whether she had paid social security contributions for the person she employed to look after her young child. It turned out that she had not and the same was the case of many other nominees. Congress then rewrote the law in order to improve enforcement. The changes made it easier to pay the contributions and increased the penalties for not doing so. Many more domestic workers were subsequently covered.

The Republic of Korea's national pension system, which previously covered 7.8 million workers, was extended in 1999 to cover a further 8.9 million persons, comprising the urban self-employed and employees of firms with fewer than five workers. The previous year the unemployment insurance scheme, initially applicable from 1995 only to employees in firms with 30 or more workers, was extended, as planned, to firms with ten or more workers; later the same year, as a result of an agreement reached in the Tripartite Commission, the scheme was further extended to workers in enterprises with five or more workers and in 1999 to part-timers.

In Spain the 1986 legislation establishing a national health service extended health care to 99.8 per cent of the population by the 1990s, bringing in all dependants of insured persons (regardless of age), recipients of social pensions and those who had previously had to have their health care financed out of poor relief.

Encouraging microinsurance and specific schemes for informal economy workers

In recent years various groups of workers in the informal economy have set up their own microinsurance schemes. In these schemes, the insurance is independently managed at the local level and sometimes the local unit links into larger structures that can enhance both the insurance function and the support structures needed for improved governance. Such schemes typically have the advantages of cohesion and direct participation, although this is not true of provider-based systems. They can also achieve low administrative costs, but views differ widely about their cost-effectiveness. They may operate within the context of a credit scheme, such as the Grameen Bank, which has already had experience with the collection of contributions and administration of payments. On the other hand, as in Argentina, mutual benefit organizations may set up credit schemes in order to subsidize their activity in the field of health care. They have in some cases developed jointly with organizations such as the Self-Employed Women's Association (SEWA) of India which have a good understanding of the needs of their members.

The term "microinsurance" refers to the ability to handle small-scale cash flows (by way of both income and expenditure), not to the size of the scheme, although often such schemes are in fact local and have a very small membership. The primary aim of many of these schemes is to help their members meet unpredictable out-of-pocket medical expenses. They do not usually aspire to provide comprehensive health insurance, still less to pay income replacement benefits.

It is estimated that these schemes usually attract about 25 per cent or less of the target population in the localities where they exist. The only schemes which manage to achieve high penetration rates (between 50 and 100 per cent) are those in particularly close-knit communities or those that all members of the target group (such as a trade union or professional association) are required to join. This percentage, though far from satisfactory, is much higher than that achieved by social insurance schemes open on a voluntary basis to all the self-employed, no doubt because microinsurance contributions are very much lower and because the schemes focus on providing only those benefits which are perceived by people as most urgently necessary.

These schemes may have the potential to increase social protection coverage substantially, by collaborating with each other and by working together with statutory social insurance schemes, local and national government and other large-scale organizations. There are various ways in which the State can promote microinsurance schemes:

- financial support: help with set-up costs, facilitating reinsurance options, payment of subsidies in the form of matching contributions, etc.;

- creation of a legislative and regulatory framework within which such schemes may operate, for example ensuring democratic and economically sound management.

It remains to validate the potential of microinsurance schemes in practice. Arguably there is justification for these schemes to receive more support and certainly they should be the subject of further research.

Examples of specific government-supported schemes for workers in the informal economy are the labour welfare schemes in India, financed from resources derived from a tax on the output of about 5 million workers in the cigarette *(beedi)* and cinema industries as well as in certain mines. A similar scheme operates in the Philippines for sugar workers. In general, however, the level of resources generated is low and only limited social protection is provided.

Introducing universal benefits or services financed from general state revenues

Universal cash benefits are to be found in a number of industrialized countries, but only rarely in developing countries, one example being Mauritius. Universal services, particularly public health services, are more common. However, in recent years the universal character of these health services has been greatly eroded by the imposition of user charges, from which only the destitute tend to be exempt.

By definition, universal schemes extend coverage to 100 per cent of the target population, for instance those over a certain age, without any contribution condition or income test. They avoid many of the problems involved in contributory systems. Naturally, they will tend to cost more to the extent that they are providing benefits to more people. However, it must be borne in mind that eligibility conditions, such as pension age, may be quite restrictive and benefit levels rather low. Universal health-care systems are able to achieve much more effective cost control than other types of health-care systems and do not need to spend money on administering systems of insurance and patient billing. Another difference between contributory schemes and universal schemes is that the latter do not provide higher cash benefits to higher earners, but a single flat-rate amount to all who qualify. This too helps to hold down the cost of universal schemes.

Universal schemes can greatly enhance gender equality. They cover people regardless of their employment status and work history, and women receive the same rate of benefit as men. The benefits typically provided by universal schemes are all of particular importance to women: old-age pensions (as women have a longer average life expectancy); child benefits (as women are typically more involved in caring for children); and health care (as the health of children and issues of reproductive health are of special concern to women).

The real problem with the existing universal schemes, which are mainly to be found in the industrialized world, is not so much their aggregate cost (which is usually less than that of contributory schemes), but the fact that — unlike contributory schemes — they have to be financed from general government revenue and therefore have to compete every year with all the government's other expenditure priorities. What may be perceived as affordable one year may be less so the next, if policies or economic conditions have changed.

The widest possible form of universal cash benefit is the citizen's income, which would be provided not only for groups such as children and the elderly — who are not expected to earn their living — but also for the able-bodied of working age. This type of proposal has excited much interest in recent years. According to some of its proponents it would replace income-tested benefits such as social assistance; for others it would replace all existing social security schemes, including social insurance.

Establishing or extending means-tested benefits or services (social assistance)

Social assistance is to be found in virtually all industrialized countries, where it serves to plug at least some of the gaps left by other social protection schemes and thus to relieve poverty. In developing countries social assistance is much less widespread. Where it exists, it is usually restricted to just one or two categories of the population, such as the elderly.

The relative paucity of social assistance schemes in the developing world testifies to the problems which many governments have in devoting adequate resources to it. This should not be seen purely as a reflection of the low absolute level of national income or of government revenue. It may be questioned whether governments, in establishing their priorities, always give sufficient weight to their social assistance schemes, whose beneficiaries are rarely in a position of political strength.

Social assistance is targeted only at those in need and the means test can in theory be made rigorous enough to exclude all but those whose needs are greatest. In practice things tend to be different, even in the most sophisticated social assistance systems. On the one hand, no means test is foolproof, so some people who are not eligible nevertheless succeed in obtaining benefits — particularly in countries where there is a thriving informal economy. Such errors are serious not only because they cost money, but above all because they undermine public confidence in the system. On the other hand, social assistance benefits fail to reach many of those in greatest need for one or more of the following reasons:

- they are unwilling to apply because of social stigma;
- they may be unaware of their rights under the legislation;
- they find it difficult to submit an application for benefit, as procedures are often complicated and time-consuming;
- social assistance is often subject to considerable administrative discretion, opening the way to favouritism, clientelism and discrimination.

The more rigorous the means test, the greater the likelihood that people will be put off from applying and that those in real need will fail to obtain benefit. Self-selection mechanisms are often more appropriate than means testing, especially in the context of developing countries. These tend to be used, for example, in the provision of paid work in labour-intensive projects and of basic food aid.

Means-tested social assistance has another major drawback, as it can discourage people from saving (or encourage dissaving) if they think that any savings they have will simply be deducted from the benefit that they would otherwise receive. Similarly, it may act as a disincentive from contributing to other forms of social protection. Thus it can help to create situations of need because of the perverse incentives inherent in means testing.

On the other hand, social assistance can be useful for specific vulnerable groups, such as the elderly and children. It may well be the only solution for widows who have not been able to contribute themselves to pension schemes or whose husbands were not covered by survivors' insurance. It is often also a way of helping poor households with children; in various countries the provision of such benefits is now linked to school attendance.

Linkages between different components of social protection

Most social protection systems are mixed and there are linkages between their different components. One obvious linkage is that certain benefits are designed to supplement others. Compulsory contributory benefits may supplement universal benefits. Voluntary contributory benefits may be intended to supplement one or both of these. The linkage between social assistance and the other components of social protection is of course quite different. If a person receiving social assistance is eligible for other social benefits, then the latter will be deducted from what would otherwise have been paid by social assistance. If these other benefits are contributory, the result is that the person has contributed for nothing.

This suggests that the relationship between means-tested schemes and contributory schemes has to be carefully thought through. Among the issues which deserve attention are: the sequence in which social assistance and contributory schemes should be established; the relative levels of benefits provided by each; and whether eligibility conditions (such as pension age) should be different. These issues give rise to real dilemmas. As policy-makers become more aware of them, they may be more prepared to give universal schemes serious consideration, in order to minimize perverse incentives.

Social protection is constantly changing and the direction in which it is likely to change is often highly dependent on what has gone before. Policy-makers should be conscious of these dynamic linkages, since otherwise the final result of their decisions may diverge significantly from their intentions. For example, they may be very keen to encourage the establishment of contributory schemes, in view of the many advantages which such schemes obviously have. However, if these schemes fail — and with non-statutory schemes in an unregulated environment this is quite likely to happen — then people's trust in such ventures may be destroyed for a long time to come. Or to take another example, tax policies may result in the establishment of voluntary contributory schemes for some workers, creating vested interests (notably among the financial institutions involved in managing them) which would stand in the way of establishing a national social security scheme covering all workers.

The existence of these various linkages serves to underline the need to develop an overall public policy concerning social protection, defining priorities and the financial involvement of the State. The key issues are to determine the institutions through which to channel state subsidies and the categories of the population which are to benefit. It is also important to recognize possible complementarities, for example, support for the creation of health-care facilities and support for the development of insurance mechanisms.

Conclusions

Those lacking social protection tend to belong to the economically weaker sections of society. The aim in the long term should be to bring them into a national system covering the whole population (or the entire labour force, as the case may be) where they can benefit from risk-pooling and solidarity. In the medium term this may be possible for middle-income developing countries, but not for the low-income countries. Such schemes are difficult to enforce, especially for some sections of the self-employed, but plans should be drawn up (and included in legislation) to extend compulsory coverage in a step-by-step manner, at least to all employees. The State may facilitate and support microinsurance schemes for those whom compulsory schemes are for the time being unable to reach, although it is clear that many of those in greatest need will never choose or be able to contribute to such schemes and will thus never benefit from any support which the State provides to them. Microinsurance schemes should be encouraged to develop in a way that will facilitate their possible integration into the national scheme and eventually the generalization of compulsory coverage.

Apart from contributory schemes, the other main types of social protection are financed from general government revenue and may take the form of means-tested or universal benefits. Governments in developing countries have been slow to develop either of these, being already under intense pressure to cut existing public expenditure, within the framework of structural adjustment programmes. However, such benefits need not be very costly: the category of persons eligible can be quite narrowly defined, at least at the initial stage, in order to limit the impact on the state budget. Over time, as the benefits prove their worth and gain political support, it should be possible to devote greater resources to them and to provide them on a less restrictive basis. Both types of benefit provided by the State can help those who are in greatest need. Universal benefits tend to cost more but they are simple to administer and they are a foundation on which individuals can build better income security for themselves and their families. They can be a powerful tool to promote gender equality and, more generally, to enhance individual autonomy, since they can free people from destitution without subjecting them to the controls and conditions usually associated with poor relief.

The goal of social protection is not mere survival, but social inclusion and the preservation of human dignity. As governments seek to extend coverage, they would do well to study the experience of countries where social security is popular and enjoys a high degree of public support. The huge task of extending social protection is one for which they will need all the public support they can get. There are no simple solutions, and the prospects of success of the various strategies will vary according to the national context. More research, accompanied by experimentation and innovation, can help to inform policy to achieve progress towards ensuring that all working people and their families enjoy decent social protection.

Chapter IV

Gender equality

Gender equality issues are to be found in virtually all aspects of social protection. While problems of unequal treatment are also dealt with in other chapters of this report, the present chapter attempts to give an overview of the topic as a whole.

The first point to emphasize is that gender equality in social protection is more than a question of securing equal treatment of men and women in the formal sense. It is also a matter of taking account, in an appropriate way, of gender roles in society, roles which differ between societies and have in recent years undergone immense change in very many countries. Thus social protection schemes should be designed, on the one hand, to guarantee equality of treatment between men and women and, on the other hand, to take into account different gender roles and serve as a tool for the promotion of gender equality.

After briefly reviewing what ILO social security Conventions and Recommendations have to say on discrimination on the basis of sex, this chapter looks at the link between social protection and gender and at the impact which labour market inequalities have on different forms of social protection. It then proceeds to consider actual and potential measures to promote gender equality through social protection.

Gender equality in social security systems is a complex matter which involves two types of discrimination, direct and indirect.

Direct discrimination can be traced to: (i) differences in treatment between economically active married women and men, based on the idea that the woman is dependent on her husband, so that her social insurance entitlements are derived rights based on his insurance rather than personal rights based on her own; (ii) differences in rates of benefits or contributions based on actuarial calculations made separately for men and women, taking into account factors such as different life expectancy, risks of morbidity and disability, anticipated work patterns, etc., such differences being found in systems of individual savings accounts in which there is no pooling of risk or solidarity.

Indirect discrimination results from measures which, although often defined without distinction as to sex, do in practice affect women and men differently because of the nature of their occupational activity, marital status or family situation. Women workers predominate in the sectors not covered by social security, such as domestic, part-time or occasional work or in the informal economy. Certain conditions, such as long qualifying periods, also penalize women.

Many women spend much of their lives outside paid employment and are thus economically dependent on their husbands. In social security systems based on gainful employment, derived rights allow a dependent spouse to benefit from health care and survivors' benefits. The issues to be considered here include: the adaptation of derived rights to changing family structures such as common-law unions, divorce and separation; the change in the concept of social protection which implies equal treatment of widows and widowers; the introduction of measures for all single parents (of which widows are but a subcategory).

International labour standards and gender equality

In the ILO's early years, standards related to women aimed primarily at protecting female workers in terms of health and safety, conditions of work and special requirements related to their reproductive function. Over time, there has been a change in the types of standards relevant to women — from protective Conventions to Conventions aimed at giving women and men equal rights and equal opportunities. The adoption of the Equal Remuneration Convention, 1951 (No. 100), the Discrimination (Employment and Occupation) Convention, 1958 (No. 111), and the Workers with Family Responsibilities Convention, 1981 (No. 156), marked a shift in traditional attitudes concerning the role of women, and a recognition that family responsibilities affect not only women workers but the family and society as well. The mid-1970s marked the emergence of a new and more ambitious concept aimed at equality of opportunity between men and women in all fields. This concept found its expression in the debates and texts that came out of the 60th Session of the International Labour Conference held in 1975. Since then the protection of working women has been based on the principle that women must be protected against the risks inherent in their job and profession on the same basis and according to the same norms as men. The special protective measures which remain permissible are those aimed at protecting women's reproductive function.

Most of the ILO social security instruments contain no provision forbidding discrimination on the basis of sex, having been adopted at a time when the prevailing opinion (often at variance with reality even then) was that men were the breadwinners and that women would normally stay at home to take care of the family. Two social security Conventions do however prohibit discrimination. One is the Maternity Protection Convention (Revised), 1952 (No. 103), which states that any contribution shall be paid in respect of all men and women employed by the enterprise without distinction on the basis of sex. The other is the Employment Promotion and Protection against Unemployment Convention, 1988 (No. 168), which requires equality of treatment for all persons protected, without discrimination on the basis inter alia of sex, while allowing member States to adopt special measures to meet the specific needs of categories of persons who have particular problems in the labour market.

Other ILO Conventions not specifically relating to social security do of course expressly prohibit discrimination on the basis of sex, namely Conventions Nos. 100,

111 and 156 mentioned above. With a view to creating effective equality of opportunity and treatment for men and women workers, Convention No. 156 prescribes that all measures compatible with national conditions and possibilities shall be taken to take account of the needs of workers with family responsibilities in social security. The Discrimination (Employment and Occupation) Recommendation, 1958 (No. 111), recommends that all persons should, without discrimination, enjoy equality of opportunity and treatment in respect of social security measures.

The protection of the reproductive function of women is intimately linked with the promotion of gender equality. Maternity insurance benefits are critical for allowing women and their families to maintain their standard of living when the mother is unable to work. Throughout its history the ILO has been concerned to ensure that women workers enjoy this entitlement, from the adoption in 1919 of the Maternity Protection Convention (No. 3) to the adoption in 2000 of the Maternity Protection Convention (No. 183) and Recommendation (No. 191).

The link between social protection and gender

Most social security schemes were initially set up on the basis of the male breadwinner model. Thus, for example, they usually provided widows' but not widowers' benefits and, in some countries, wives who engaged in paid employment did not have to contribute to the scheme. A lower pensionable age for women was also in some ways a reflection of a model in which the labour force participation of women was regarded as secondary. As more and more women have joined the paid labour force, ideas about gender roles have evolved and social security schemes are gradually being reformed.

Within social protection there are two complementary approaches leading towards gender equality:

● prescriptions/measures to level the playing field and ensure that equal treatment is granted to men and women. The goal is to eliminate discriminatory practices in programme design; but women remain in a disadvantaged position in terms of social protection as long as social security benefits are tied to labour market employment, where pervasive gender inequalities persist;

● prescriptions/measures to equalize outcomes and compensate for discrimination and inequalities generated outside the social security systems, for example in the labour market.

The impact of labour market inequalities on different forms of social protection

Women are often in a disadvantaged position in the labour market. Their situation is determined by the division of labour, in which they undertake a very large share of unpaid caring work. The latter role often prevents women from taking up or remaining in full-time employment. It affects the type of work they can undertake and the number of years they spend in employment covered by social security. It

71

often has an adverse effect on their earnings, on their ability to pursue their training and on their prospects for professional advancement. Even women who currently have no caring responsibilities may be affected, if employers assume that they will have in future.

These labour market inequalities affect the position of women in some types of social protection much more than others. Some of the strongest effects are to be seen in company pension and health plans: women are more often excluded from these schemes than men, because they are in lower grades, or have insufficient years of service, or work part time. Company schemes also exclude those workers who, for one reason or another, are not covered by social insurance schemes. Company schemes provide benefits that are related to the level of previous earnings and to length of service, both factors which tend to favour men. In addition, some are final pay schemes, which are particularly advantageous for employees who have moved up most in the company and for those who have long periods of uninterrupted service. Again this is more likely to be the case for men than for women.

All sorts of savings schemes for old age tend to reflect, and indeed to amplify, labour market inequalities. Workers in low-paid and precarious jobs, among whom women are disproportionately represented, cannot afford to save much and often fail to do so, even in countries where the law has supposedly made retirement savings schemes mandatory. Those whose savings are small or irregular typically get a lower net return, as a greater proportion of their savings is eaten up by administrative costs, owing to the higher costs of small accounts. In savings systems there is no solidarity or redistribution. Because of their greater life expectancy, women's pensions are lower than those of men, even if their savings are of the same value.

Social insurance schemes frequently do not cover categories such as homeworkers, domestic workers and part-time workers, in which women are heavily represented. Workers in the informal economy — where so many women spend much of their working life — are also unprotected. Interrupted careers, shorter contribution records and lower pay adversely affect women's entitlements under social insurance as in other employment-related schemes. This affects not only pensions but also unemployment benefits, which many unemployed women do not receive. (If they are single they may be able to obtain social assistance benefits, but these are usually lower and subject to numerous restrictions. If they have a partner, the household means test usually disqualifies them from social assistance, as explained below.) However, social insurance schemes do have certain features which attenuate labour market inequalities, such as minimum pensions or weighted benefit formulae favouring the lower paid.

For workers in the informal economy, notably in developing countries, microinsurance schemes can help to fill the gap in social protection, and some of them cater especially for women; given the voluntary character of such schemes, however, there tends to be little systematic redistribution from men to women.

Universal schemes — national health services, child benefits, universal old-age benefits — usually give women the same rights as men, regardless of employment and earnings history. As noted in Chapter III, they can greatly enhance gender equality.

As for social assistance schemes, these may, in formal terms, provide for equality of treatment and, since they cater for the poor, tend to redistribute income in favour of women (at least to those who are single). However, social assistance benefits are means-tested against the earnings of a spouse or partner; given that men usually have higher earnings than women, the result in practice is likely to be that a married woman has less chance of receiving benefit than a married man. And where a male partner succeeds in establishing entitlement to social assistance, the element of the benefit intended to meet the needs of his female partner will be paid to him, not to the woman.

Finally, it should be borne in mind that not only do labour market inequalities affect social protection, but social protection also has an impact on labour market inequalities. For example, a well-functioning system of unemployment benefits (including both unemployment insurance and unemployment assistance for those without insurance entitlements) helps to minimize the problems of low-paid, low-productivity jobs. Childcare and other social services are also of crucial importance in helping women to compete in the labour market on a more equal footing with men.

Measures to grant equality of treatment in social protection and to promote gender equality through social protection

A wide range of social protection measures have been used or may potentially be used to promote gender equality. These and some other issues relevant to gender equality are examined below under the following headings:

- survivors' pensions;
- divorce and pension-splitting;
- pensionable age;
- pension credits for persons with caring responsibilities;
- sex-differentiated annuity rates;
- parental leave and benefits and childcare services;
- child benefit.

Survivors' pensions

Survivors' pensions are based on the notion of dependency: they link benefit entitlements to the contributions paid by (or on behalf of) the deceased spouse, they insure against the loss of the breadwinner and (in many countries) they may be suspended if the recipient remarries. Traditionally survivors' benefits were provided only to the widow and to orphans, not to the widower (unless he had a disability and was for that reason dependent on his wife). This discrimination has been abolished in the social security systems of many countries, including the United States and most Member States of the European Union. Discrimination against widowers was ruled to be unlawful in occupational pension schemes by the European Court of Justice in 1993.

Mainly as a result of the developments described above, elements of income testing have been introduced in the statutory survivors' benefits schemes, for example in France, Greece, Italy, the Netherlands and Sweden. Other countries have restricted the payment of benefit to survivors above a certain age (at which it is judged to be difficult to enter employment) and to those caring for young children. As a result of such restrictions, some women are worse off than they would have been under the old legislation. Those who are younger than the specified age may experience real difficulty finding employment. And even for many who are employed, the death of the husband may lead to serious financial difficulties, if no widow's pension is payable: the household budget in most cases is then less than half of what it was. The main aim of these restrictive measures has been to limit the increase in the cost of survivors' benefits resulting from their extension to widowers. It is no doubt significant that equal treatment of survivors was introduced at a time when social security systems already faced financial problems. The issue has given rise to a debate between those who feel it is reasonable that women should nowadays normally be expected to earn their living and those who point out that this was not what was expected of many women entering married life in past decades. Should those becoming widows now suffer because values and attitudes have changed?

In numerous pension systems, women who are not legally married do not qualify for a survivor's pension upon the death of their partner. However, some countries do grant a pension provided that there is evidence of dependency or cohabitation. Such is the case, for example, in Costa Rica, Denmark, Luxembourg, the Netherlands, Norway, the United Kingdom and Venezuela.

The position of widows in developing countries, particularly in Africa and South Asia, is very much more difficult than in the industrialized economies, not only because the social security systems are more rudimentary, but also because widows are often subject to discrimination, social isolation and even physical violence. If a country has a universal pension (or a social assistance pension available on conditions that are not too restrictive), this is of immense assistance to older widows, few of whom will have any contributory entitlements whatsoever. However, it should be remembered that many widows are not nearly old enough to qualify for an old-age pension, particularly in societies with a tradition of child brides and in countries seriously affected by AIDS and by wars. (High mortality rates from AIDS, among both men and women, are also leaving many orphans, most of whom have no benefit entitlements.) Various states in India have extended means-tested pensions to cover destitute widows, but problems of implementation have limited the impact of such measures.

Divorce and pension splitting

The last three or four decades of the twentieth century saw a rapid rise in the rate of divorce in many industrialized countries. For example, in both Canada and the United Kingdom they were six times higher in 1990 than in 1960. Between the mid-1970s and the mid-1990s the rate doubled in the Republic of Korea, Thailand and Venezuela. This trend has profound implications for the old-age security of divorced women, particularly where they have not themselves been in pensionable employment. If the former husband remarries — as is most often the case — they may lose some or all of their entitlement to a widow's pension.

To deal with this problem, pension systems in various countries have introduced a refinement commonly known as "pension splitting". All the pension entitlements earned by both partners while they were married to each other are added up, then divided equally between them. Such a system has existed in the social security schemes of Canada and Germany for almost a quarter of a century. More recently, it has been introduced in Ireland, South Africa and Switzerland. It has recently also attracted attention in relation to occupational pension schemes.

Pensionable age

Numerous countries either have or have had until recently a lower pensionable age for women than for men, as shown in table 4.1. Why did legislators in these countries (the overwhelming majority of whom were men) decide to make this difference? It has been suggested that it may be related to the tendency for men to marry somewhat younger women and for them to wish to retire about the same time. Another possible explanation is that the age for women is lower to compensate for the double burden they have borne, by going out to work and also doing most of the work in the home.

A lower pensionable age for women constitutes formal discrimination against men. The difference, where it still exists, is now widely questioned. That women do bear a double burden is undeniably true, but whether this affects their ability to remain in employment until the same age as men is far from evident. Indeed their higher life expectancy might even suggest the opposite. A consensus is tending to emerge in favour of a common pensionable age, as already exists in Canada, France, Germany, Japan, the United States and many other countries. However, what that age should be is often the subject of heated debate. Many women are understandably reluctant to see their pensionable age increase or to receive reduced pensions at the existing pensionable age. On the other hand, if the age for men were to be reduced, the cost would be enormous. This would in any case be inadvisable, since the projected rise in the ratio of pensioners to workers suggests that pensionable age should rise rather than fall.

Many countries which are increasing pensionable age have introduced an element of flexibility that allows workers to continue drawing their pension from the previous pensionable age, subject to an actuarial reduction. Generally speaking, women have opposed proposals to increase their pensionable age and/or to reduce

Table 4.1.   Differences in standard pensionable ages for men and women, 1999

Country	Men	Women
Algeria	60	55
Armenia	62	57
Australia	65	61.5 (rising to 65 by 2013)
Austria	65	60
Belgium	65	61 (rising to 65 by 2009)
Brazil	65	60
Bulgaria	60	55
Chile	65	60
China	60	50; 55 (if salaried); 60 (if professional)
Colombia	60	55
Cuba	60	55
Hungary	60 (62 by 2009)	57 (rising to 62 by 2009)
Iran, Islamic Rep. of	60	55
Iraq	60	55
Israel	65	60 (65 for housewives)
Italy (old law, for persons working before 1996)	64	59
Pakistan	60	55
Poland	65	60
Romania	60	55
Russian Federation	60	55
Slovakia	60	53-57 (according to number of children raised)
Slovenia	63	58
South Africa	65	60
Sudan	60	55
Switzerland	65	62 (rising to 64 by 2005)
Turkey	55	50
Ukraine	60	55
United Kingdom	65	60 (rising to 65 by 2020)
Uruguay	60	56 (rising to 60 by 2003)
Venezuela	60	55
Viet Nam	60	55

Source: United States Social Security Administration: *Social Security Programs throughout the World,* 1999 (Washington, DC, 1999).

the benefits granted at the existing pensionable age. However, some women work-ers may stand to gain, if the increase means that they can stay longer than before in employment and build up bigger pension entitlements. For women who have taken time out of the labour force to raise a family, this may be a real advantage, assuming of course that they do wish to carry on working and that they are actually obliged to retire at the standard pensionable age. To be regarded as equitable, increases in pensionable age usually have to be introduced gradually. For example, a formula commonly suggested in Central and Eastern European countries has been to raise the age each year by three months — thereby phasing in a five-year increase over a 20-year period. This is necessary, not only to give the working population time to adjust to quite a profound change, but also to allow time for the labour market to adjust: a more rapid increase could lead to significantly higher unemployment.

Pension credits for persons with caring responsibilities

Many women reach retirement age with low or even zero pension entitlements in their own right — either because their unpaid work as carers has prevented them from participating in the paid labour force or because their caring responsibilities have obliged them to participate only in peripheral forms of employment, which are poorly remunerated and not covered by social security systems. In order to help remedy this problem, numerous countries have introduced provisions under which persons staying at home to care for young children (and for others unable to look after themselves) are awarded pension credits for the period in question as if they had been employed and paying social security contributions. Among the countries with such provisions are Germany, Norway, Sweden and Switzerland. Ireland and the United Kingdom have implemented a variant of the caring credit through a procedure called home responsibilities protection which provides for years of low or zero earnings to be disregarded in the calculation of the pension amount. In 1996 Ireland increased the number of years for which such protection could be available by raising the age of qualifying children from six to 12. These measures contribute to gender equality not only as they help to provide better income security for the many women who leave the labour force to raise a family, but also as they are available to husbands who look after the children while their wives pursue their careers. Another approach, which in practice helps more to promote labour market equality, is the provision of childcare services.

Sex-differentiated annuity rates

In most of the mandatory retirement savings systems that have been introduced to date, particularly in Latin America, workers upon retirement have the option between the purchase of an annuity and a phased withdrawal of the money in their account. Under this type of system — unlike the existing social insurance schemes — there is no pooling of risk or solidarity between men and women (who have a substantially longer average life expectancy). Hungary and Poland, however, have provided in their legislation for mandatory lifetime annuities using unisex rates. It remains to be seen how easy it will be to enforce such legislation upon competitive annuity companies, all of which will have a strong preference for male customers. The male/female pension differentials in the Latin American countries concerned may be widened not only by the introduction of gender-specific parameters, such as lower annuity rates for women, but also perhaps by the increase in the standard pensionable age for women and the associated actuarial reductions for women unwilling or unable to postpone retirement.

Parental leave and benefits and childcare services

Social security can promote gender equality not only by compensating unpaid carers for lost periods of pensionable employment, but also by making it easier for either men or women to assume the caring role and for them to do so without abandoning their careers. Parental leave and parental benefits (which replace their lost earnings) contribute significantly to this objective:

● as they are available to the mother or the father or can be shared by both;

● as they usually also provide for a number of days per year on which either parent may take time off work to look after a child who is sick.

The provision of high-quality and affordable childcare services, often under the aegis of social security institutions or social service agencies, also plays an important role in promoting gender equality. The need for these services has risen as the participation of women in paid work has increased. In many countries a higher proportion of the workforce is faced with the competing demands of work and family responsibilities.

Child benefit

Child benefit is also a measure that favours gender equality in more ways than one. It is a benefit that is nowadays usually paid to the parent effectively caring for the child. This is an important consideration as the distribution of income within the single-breadwinner family is often highly unequal and breadwinners sometimes abuse the dominant position that receipt of the household income confers. While common in industrialized countries, child benefits are to be found in very few developing countries.

Recent years have seen a large rise in the proportion of families that are headed by a lone parent. Since 1960 this has more than doubled in countries such as the United Kingdom and the United States. This trend is related to the enormous increase in births to unmarried mothers (up more than fivefold in these and other countries), as well as to rising divorce rates. The vast majority of lone parents are women, most of them young. Given the high cost of childcare in many countries and the limited access of young mothers to reasonably well-paid jobs, many of those concerned find that they have little choice but to stay at home with the child and live on social assistance or other means-tested benefits. But if child benefit is paid, this can, in combination with earnings from employment, provide them with a viable alternative. For those who are trying to develop a career and are often at an early and crucial stage, having the option to enter or remain in employment may be extremely important for their future earnings potential.

In developing countries the provision of child benefit conditional upon school attendance can be a powerful instrument for ensuring that both girls and boys receive an education and for combating the scourge of child labour. Such benefits can take the form of waivers of school fees, which is probably the most powerful incentive for children to go to school. The experience with cash grants to families and children shows that they are a useful initial incentive for families to withdraw their children from work and send them to school. If possible these should be reinforced by other provisions such as school lunches, books, uniforms, pads and pencils, transport, accommodation and counselling, which encourage children to attend school and to remain in school. The *Bolsa Escola* programme in Brazil, for example, has shown how cash grants can help very poor families to keep their children in school. Its major impact is to allow poor children to remain in school when they would otherwise be excluded owing to inadequate academic performance. Although only a minute number of families has benefited so far from the programme and the amount they receive does not eliminate poverty, in-depth assessments have indicated a significant impact on beneficiary families.

Conclusions

Reflecting the opinions prevailing at the time of their adoption, most ILO social security Conventions contain no prohibition of discrimination on the basis of sex, although certain other ILO instruments touch briefly upon the subject.

Social security can enhance gender equality by:

- extending coverage to all workers, or at least to all employees, including the particular categories in which women are heavily represented;

- helping men and women to combine paid employment and caring work, for example through paid parental leave and child benefits;

- recognizing unpaid caring work either through the award of credits under contributory schemes or through the provision of universal benefits;

- granting dependent spouses entitlements in their own right, thereby safeguarding their position in case of separation or divorce.

The introduction of gender equality with regard to parameters such as pensionable age or survivors' benefits may, however, have an adverse effect on women, as it can lead to a levelling down of entitlements, rather than a levelling up. Where, for economic or other reasons, this is judged to be unavoidable, there must at least be a careful and gradual transition process.

Finally, all social security reforms should be closely scrutinized for possible adverse implications for women and for gender equality.

Chapter V

The financing of social security

Many contemporary national social security systems — financed largely on a pay-as-you-go (PAYG) basis — are presently criticized on the grounds that they will become unaffordable, inefficient or ineffective in the face of ageing populations, or owing to the competitive forces in the new global economy and to the growth of the informal economy. The main point made in this chapter is that affordability of social protection will remain much more a question of national income policy preferences than of objective economic circumstance. There may be social transfer levels that some countries cannot afford, but very few are too poor to share enough resources at least to avoid destitution. However, globalization will require new policy responses.

Global trends in social security expenditure

Worldwide social security expenditure has been on the increase for decades. In market economy countries sharp increases were observed in the *overall social expenditure ratio* (i.e. social security expenditure measured as a percentage of GDP) in the 1960s and 1970s, followed by a stagnation during the second half of the 1980s and most of the 1990s. Social security expenditure reached an average of about 18 per cent in the mid-1990s in the OECD countries (25 per cent in the EU Member States). In the former planned economies, economic transition placed a heavy strain on the badly prepared social transfer systems during the 1990s, yet total social security expenditure was maintained at about 15 to 20 per cent (excluding subsidies on certain goods and services) — albeit of contracting levels of GDP. In the developing world the picture is more heterogeneous. As a general rule expenditure has increased in recent decades. But it grew from a level which on the whole was about ten times lower than in developed countries in the 1960s and is still three to five times lower. Table 5.1 shows aggregate worldwide and regional levels of social security expenditure in 1990, the most recent year for which fairly complete data are available.[1] The social expenditure ratio is an aggregate measure and does not reveal how the redistributed resources are allocated equitably to specific population groups or whether they are allocated efficiently. However, it is useful as an indicator of general trends.

---

[1] For more detailed data, see the statistical annex at the end of this report.

Table 5.1.   Aggregate levels of social security expenditure, 1990

Region[1]	Total social security expenditure (% of GDP)	Of which: Pensions	Health care
All countries	14.5	6.6	4.9
Africa	4.3	1.4	1.7
Asia	6.4	3.0	2.7
Europe	24.8	12.1	6.3
Latin America and the Caribbean	8.8	2.1	2.8
North America	16.6	7.1	7.5
Oceania	16.1	4.9	5.6

[1] Averages refer only to countries for which data are available. For the countries included in each region, see the statistical annex at the end of this report.
Source: *World Labour Report 2000,* op. cit., statistical annex, table 14.

Under status quo conditions it is to be expected that formal social expenditure will continue to increase for some time. Schemes in developing countries will mature, their scope will expand and new schemes will be introduced. In the more developed economies overall social security expenditure could grow further if dependency ratios were to continue to rise. Dependency will remain high or will increase further if female labour force participation in some major economies remains relatively low (compared to that of males), if the average age of entry into the labour market continues to rise and if de facto retirement ages continue to drop.

It is often maintained that there is a simple relationship between social security expenditure and GDP levels. In other words, as countries get richer they tend to spend more on social security. Figure 5.1 shows that this is only partly true. It approaches the problem through a straightforward two-dimensional regression. While the exercise may be methodologically simple, it produces some interesting results.

The graph indicates that the mathematical correlation between GDP per capita and social security expenditure as a percentage of GDP is relatively weak (even using a non-linear, i.e. exponential, regression line).[2] However, it also reveals a more complex picture. The advanced industrialized countries clearly have a higher level of transfers through the social protection system than lower-income countries. The higher- and lower-income countries actually form two clusters around the regression line. However, neither cluster is very dense. This means that the level of social security spending varies substantially between countries with similar GDP per capita. Clearly, the level of social expenditure (measured as a percentage of GDP) does not — at least exclusively — depend on the level of GDP. Thus there are poorer societies which decide to devote a similar percentage of their GDP to social security expenditure to that spent by societies which are far better off. This indicates that social spending is also to a large extent a matter of political choice.

---

[2] The R square measure is only 0.2858, which is not normally taken to indicate a measurable correlation.

Social security and its main challenges

Contemporary social protection financing systems face three major challenges. They are said to be ill-equipped to deal with the ageing of the population and with globalization, and the financial burden placed on contributors and taxpayers in all countries is said to have reached the limits of affordability. This section briefly analyses the arguments, then sets out the options at the national and international levels to deal with the challenges.

Figure 5.1. **Relationship between social security expenditure (as a percentage of GDP) and GDP per capita (in thousand US$), selected countries, mid-1990s**

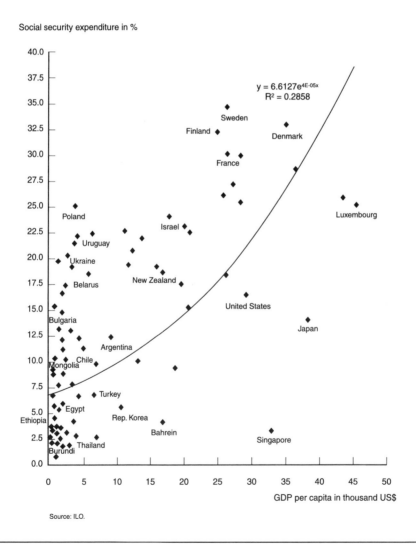

Social security expenditure in %

$$y = 6.6127e^{4E\text{-}05x}$$
$$R^2 = 0.2858$$

GDP per capita in thousand US$

Source: ILO.

Does social security face an ageing crisis?

Ageing — often misrepresented as the key challenge for the financing of formal social transfer systems — will pose a major problem only if rapidly ageing societies cannot contain overall social dependency. However, even in Europe — where the ageing process is at a relatively advanced stage — dependency could be reduced substantially through increased retirement ages and greater labour force participation of women. An ageing society need not face any crisis, as long as it is able to provide jobs for its ageing workforce. After decades of heavy investment in health care through social protection, people are remaining fit and healthy until later in life and should be able to work longer. In addition, modern and more flexible lifetime working patterns should be able to accommodate employment patterns needed by parents and older workers. ILO model calculations show that in a typical rapidly ageing European country with a de facto retirement age of 60 and a female labour force participation rate like that of the Netherlands, the combined unemployment and old-age pensioner dependency ratio would have been on the order of 62 dependants per 100 employed persons in 1995. If the country were to (a) raise the de facto retirement age to 67 by 2030 and (b) increase female labour force participation to the present highest levels in Europe (i.e. the Swedish level) then the combined dependency ratio in 2030 would amount to about 68 per 100 employed. Under status quo conditions (i.e. unchanged de facto retirement age of 60 and unchanged labour force participation of women) that ratio would be 80 to 100, or about 18 per cent higher. Employment is the key to the future financing of social protection in all societies. Ageing is not so much a threat for social security systems as a challenge for economic and social policy-making and for the labour market.

Or does social security face a globalization crisis?

The statistical annex shows that up to now some of the countries with the most open economies have the highest levels of social spending (for example, most of the Nordic countries, Austria, Germany, the Netherlands). Open national economies in a global economy do not have to have lower social spending. On the contrary, a higher level of social protection would appear to be necessary in countries that are more exposed to external risks or which have to undergo difficult structural adjustments.

However, the data reflect economic realities in the mid-1990s. In the meantime political realities appear to have changed to some extent. Globalization not only channels liquid financial resources from one part of the world to another, it also exposes whole industries to new competitive pressures; pressures which subsequently trickle down — as pressures on wages and non-wage labour costs — to employees. Credible threats to relocate enterprises or actual closures due to competitive forces can in practice limit the power of the nation State to tax or collect contributions.

National fiscal policies may react by seeking to move to income sources which are not exposed to globalization pressures or do not negatively affect the country's competitive position, or by taking measures to curb expenditures in systems that are seen to affect labour costs. Containing overall labour costs is an explicit policy objective in most highly industrialized countries as well as many developing countries. There is wide agreement among economists that social security contributions and taxes are not driving labour costs.[3] Labour markets determine the price of the overall compensation package of employees. Nevertheless, since wages — the major component of that package — are often hard to change directly, the labour cost debate often concentrates on other elements of labour costs, notably on social insurance contributions. If alternative sources of financing cannot be found, benefit levels in public social security schemes tend to be reduced.

The diminishing fiscal sovereignty of the nation State as a result of globalization is one of the major new challenges for national social protection systems.

Has social security reached the limits of its affordability?

It is the case in all societies (assuming the intention to treat their members with decency) that income is shared, to a greater or lesser extent and by more or less transparent means, between those who have the capacity to earn it and those who are unable to do so. However, the levels of transfers recorded in national statistics do not appear to correspond very closely to the economic potential of different countries. This suggests that the measurement of transfers, in most countries, is very inexact. In countries where extended family and kinship structures remain relatively strong, these may well provide the major vehicles for transfers, on an informal basis, whereas other countries have moved towards more formal redistributive mechanisms, such as national pension schemes. Overall, it seems certain that the differentials between countries in total (informal and formal) transfers are much smaller than shown in national and international social statistics.

A simple quantitative exercise may illustrate the point. It is assumed here that the economically active population (including the unemployed) earn all the income in a country (i.e. profits and wages) and would share this income with children, inactive persons in the active age group and persons beyond active age. It is assumed also that the ratio of consumption of an active person to that of an economically inactive person (in any decent society) is 1 to 0.666.[4] Based on these assumptions a hypothetical transfer ratio can be calculated for selected regions. Figure 5.2 displays the estimated total transfer ratio and also compares the estimated extent of informal transfers to the statistically known extent of formal transfers.

One has to bear in mind that this exercise is to some extent speculative, as the data basis is far from perfect. However, it appears that worldwide, only about half of the total transfers are presently channelled through formal social protection sys-

---

[3] *World Labour Report 2000,* op. cit., p. 68.

[4] This is of course a hypothetical assumption; it is assumed implicitly that the overall degree of sharing of consumption is independent of the relative proportions of those dependent by reason of childhood and those dependent by reason of old age.

Figure 5.2.   Estimated total transfers and their composition in selected regions, early 1990s (as percentage of GDP)

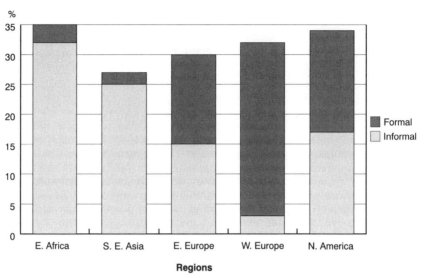

Source: ILO estimates.

tems. Most of these formal transfers are taking place in Europe. In the developing world only a small fraction of total transfers is channelled through formal systems. For the time being the overwhelming part of all transfers in these societies is still achieved by informal arrangements. The total transfer ratios calculated show that the formal social protection expenditure projected for even the Western European countries is smaller than the total estimated transfers.

It can be concluded that most countries (except possibly the poorest) are redistributing more societal resources than formal social transfer statistics indicate. There is no reason to believe that formal social transfer levels have anywhere become excessive in terms of the income redistribution which societies find necessary. The debate on the affordability of social protection is thus really a debate on policy preferences for particular redistribution mechanisms.

National financing options

Each country has to adapt its overall social protection financing systems to its economic circumstances, its demographic situation and — most importantly — the preferences of its citizens. Each country has a limited set of possible transfer mechanisms at its disposal, ranging from completely informal intra-family transfers to universal systems financed from general government revenue, with many intermediate possibilities. National policy choices and objectives are embodied in the selected financing systems and the role of governments versus the private provision of social transfers. This section attempts to discern these often implicit choices and objectives.

Financing systems

Financing systems can be described in terms of the following parameters:

- the extent of group solidarity;
- the level and pattern of funding; and
- the sources of financing.

The extent of group solidarity

The smallest group within which transfers occur is obviously the nuclear family. The next smallest group is the extended family or the immediate neighbourhood, followed by the community or by occupational groups. Unless mandated by specific legal provisions (such as alimony provisions in family law), transfers within families and/or small communities are most often of an informal nature. The extent of solidarity within these groups varies greatly, depending on values and on specific family or community circumstances. There are often no clear entitlements to benefits, even in community-based schemes. Just as in informal family settings, community-based transfer levels often depend on the level of income of the group as a whole rather than on the precise needs of potential transfer recipients.

The theory of insurance suggests that the viability of a scheme increases with the size of the insured group. National schemes or social insurance schemes with a wide coverage generally have more stable income than schemes restricted to smaller groups. The variance of the benefit experience of large groups (i.e. their financial risk) is inevitably more stable than that of smaller groups, which in turn stabilizes their financial position. Small groups also often face joint risks, such as unemployment in an occupational group, poverty in a family, or epidemics in a community. In other words larger schemes can usually cope better with most risks, provided they are well governed. The disaggregation of national solidarity into smaller solidarity groups inevitably leads to a wider disparity of benefit levels. In various parts of the world, a trend may be observed towards greater disaggregation of solidarity groups, the extreme case being that of individual accounts. This inevitably creates greater benefit inequalities and uncertainties.

The level and pattern of funding

Short-term benefit schemes (with the notable exception of private health insurance schemes) are generally financed on a PAYG basis on all levels of group risk-pooling. The rationale is that short-term benefits are short-term promises and can be adapted relatively quickly to changing demographic or economic circumstances and hence do not need to build up huge reserves for distant future liabilities. In the case of pension schemes three financing methods are commonly distinguished:

- PAYG, i.e. virtually no advance funding;
- full advance funding; and
- intermediate or partial funding.

Private pension systems usually are fully funded, i.e. they have to have sufficient resources to honour their obligations should the insurance company, the occupational pension scheme or the sponsor of an occupational scheme be dissolved. If this condition is met, the scheme is fully funded. Public pension schemes, which are backed by a societal promise guaranteeing their liquidity and — ideally — indefinite existence, do not require the same level of funding. The level of funding in social security schemes is determined by considerations other than the exclusive financial safeguarding of pension promises. Most social security pension systems are in practice partially funded. Even systems which were originally designed to be fully funded often became partially funded when inflation undermined the value of reserves. Recently several countries with old PAYG schemes have begun to introduce defined contribution funded second-tier schemes (Hungary, Latvia, Poland). Others are introducing reserve funds in their PAYG schemes (e.g. Canada, France and the Netherlands). From a purely financial point of view, there is no real difference between a partially funded defined benefit scheme and a pension system which consists of an unfunded and a funded tier. In aggregate terms, both are partially funded.

Recent years have seen an intense international debate on the merits or demerits of increased advance funding of national pension schemes. While social security pension schemes do not really require the financial security that a high level of funding may provide for small private systems, extraneous reasons for advance funding

Table 5.2. National savings rates (1990-92) and occupational pension assets (1990-91)

Country	National savings (as % of GDP)	Pension assets (as % of GNP)
Australia	18	39
Canada	15	35
Denmark	19	60
France	21	3
Germany	23	4
Ireland	20	37
Japan	34	8
Netherlands	25	76
Switzerland	30	70
United Kingdom	14	73
United States	15	66

Note: The savings rate is the total (private sector plus government) savings rate.

Source: Gerard Hughes: "Pension financing, the substitution effect and national savings", in Gerard Hughes and Jim Stewart (eds.): *Pensions in the European Union: Adapting to economic and social change* (Dordrecht, Kluwer, 2000).

of pension schemes are frequently invoked. Funding, it is claimed, can increase national savings. As shown in table 5.2, the evidence does not support that contention. High levels of national savings may well coincide with low levels of pension reserves and vice versa. Funding is often said to stimulate the growth of capital markets. But, here again, the evidence is far from compelling: emerging stock markets have notched up very impressive growth rates in various countries where there are few, if any, funded pension schemes.

It is often claimed that funding will help to insulate pension schemes against the negative effects of ageing. While this is possibly true for small insured communities within a society or a small country in a global economy, the same does not apply to whole national societies or to global society as a whole. A society has to allocate a certain amount of resources to provide a certain level of consumption for its elderly. The shift from wage-based to capital-based financing does not change that fundamental equation. Ultimately the consumption of the retired population has to be financed out of the current GDP produced by the active population (unless it sells real assets to the rest of the world).

It must be expected that advance funded and PAYG financed pension schemes will both be vulnerable to demographic change. Funded schemes operate on the principle that pensioners are able in effect to sell their assets to (or use them as collateral to borrow from) active generations in order to generate cash income. If the buyer generation contracts, then one must expect asset prices to drop, thereby reducing the retirement income of the selling generation.

A heavy strain on national finances (as opposed to the real amount of transfers needed to finance the consumption of the elderly) may arise if a country moves from PAYG financing to advance funding (for example by replacing its social insurance scheme wholly or partially with private funding arrangements), as a (long) transitional period will be necessary during which funds must be accumulated by current workers to finance future pensions while at the same time pensions must be paid to current pensioners. There is then a real risk that the value of the social insurance benefits may be allowed to fall, in order to achieve economies and to limit the amounts that government would otherwise have to raise through taxation or borrowing or the sale of assets.

If funding per se does not increase the resources that can be allocated to the dependent population and economic advantages of funding are uncertain, then the only policy rationale for switching from PAYG defined benefit schemes to funded defined contribution schemes (as in Latin America and parts of Eastern Europe) lies in the stabilization of social security contribution or tax rates. As benefit levels are then dependent on long-term capital market performance, certainty concerning contribution or tax levels is achieved at the cost of uncertain benefit levels. This represents a complete reversal of previous policy objectives.

Sources of financing

National social security systems are generally financed through the following main sources of revenue:

- social security contributions paid by employers and/or workers;

- taxes, which may be either part of general government revenue or earmarked taxes;

- investment income; and

- private out-of-pocket outlays or insurance premiums.

However, most national social security systems are in practice financed by a mix of sources (see table 5.3). This even applies to subsystems such as pension schemes.

The present debate about high public spending on social protection may disguise the fact that many government budgets have substantially benefited from the existence of national social security schemes. Young pension schemes and unemployment benefit schemes during periods of high growth normally produce large surpluses when contributions are collected but no or few pensions are paid. These surpluses might have simply been absorbed into the general government budget either through straight transfers (as was the case in Central and Eastern Europe) or through lending (as was the case in many African schemes). Many of these transfers were never returned and low interest rates (often negative in real terms) were paid on the loans. In such cases, social security contributions were thus to a large extent another form of taxation.

Table 5.3. Current contribution rates in national social security pension schemes, selected countries

Scheme	Total rate of contribution (as % of total insurable earnings)	Employer share (%)	Employee share (%)	Government contribution
Belgium	16.36	8.86	7.5	Annual subsidies
France	14.75	8.2	6.55	Variable subsidies
Gabon	7.5	5	2.5	None
Germany	19.5	9.75	9.75	Cost of non-insurance benefits
Italy	32.7	23.81	8.89	Cost of social assistance benefit plus overall deficit
Korea, Rep. of	9	4.5	4.5	Partial cost of administration
Luxembourg	24	8	8	8% of insurable earnings
Pakistan	5	5	None	Subsidies as needed
Poland	32.52 (including invalidity)	16.26	16.26	Funds for minimum pension guarantee
Trinidad and Tobago	8.4	5.6	2.8	Full cost of social assistance benefits
United States	12.4	6.2	6.2	Cost of special benefits and means-tested allowance

Source: United States Social Security Administration, op. cit.

89

Figure 5.3.   Social expenditure as a percentage of GDP, 1995

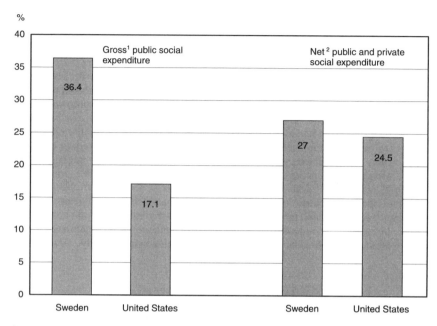

¹ Before taxes.
² After taxes.

Source: Willem Adema: *Net social expenditure*, Labour market and social policy occasional papers No. 39 (Paris, OECD, 1999).

Governments often feel unable to finance social protection expenditure from general tax revenue. The traditional solution has been to provide special legislation for social security to be financed from compulsory contributions which have to be used only for the purposes specified in the legislation. However, governments may also explicitly mandate private agencies to finance and provide social security, or they may choose to leave any such provision up to voluntary initiative. Private provision, mandatory or voluntary, is often regarded as a convenient way of keeping down public expenditure (broadly defined to include social security expenditure financed from contributions). It is, however, incorrect to think that private provision has no effect on public finances. There is an obvious indirect linkage between all public and private social protection financing instruments. In addition to the contingent liabilities of the government as ultimate guarantor of most social transfers, that linkage is defined by the overall limit of aggregate social charges (both public and private) that is accepted by the population. It seems probable that most people, if obliged to make payments on a mandatory basis, will be indifferent — subject to equivalent guarantees — as to whether these take the form of contributions (or taxes) to a public institution or premiums to private institutions. They are prepared to accept a certain aggregate level of social charges in return for a certain level of protection. If charges increase beyond the acceptable level, tax avoidance strategies begin to take their toll on public revenues. There is no general rule as to what combined level of social security contributions and taxes is acceptable. This has to be tested on a trial and error basis in long-term political consensus-building processes.

However, there are indications that the differences between countries — at least between countries at the same level of development — are less pronounced than commonly assumed. The point is illustrated in figure 5.3, which compares social expenditure (as a percentage of GDP) in two advanced industrialized economies, Sweden and the United States. While gross public social expenditure is twice as large in Sweden as in the United States, net total social expenditure is of roughly the same order of magnitude in both countries. The explanation is twofold: a relatively large part of social expenditure in the United States, particularly on health care and pensions, is private, and in Sweden a comparatively large share of public social expenditure is recouped in taxes. While the net total spent in the two countries is about the same, the results are radically different in social terms, mainly because private social expenditure is much more unequally distributed than public.

The indispensable role of government as ultimate financial guarantor

In addition to assuming direct financial costs on a regular basis, governments may bear indirect costs or be liable for potential costs. Governments play an important role as financial guarantor, or ultimate underwriter, of social security schemes or even of privately administered social security systems.[5] The liabilities of governments can take several explicit and implicit forms. An explicit liability exists when the social insurance law stipulates that the government will cover any deficit of the scheme. Guarantee payments of this type exist in several countries, both in Western Europe and in Central and Eastern Europe (for example, Bulgaria). Governments also have an explicit liability when the State guarantees a minimum benefit, by supplementing pensions falling below that level for any beneficiary fulfilling prescribed conditions. The magnitude of such contingent liabilities may be considerably affected by systemic declines in the rate of return on pension assets and by market turmoil-induced falls in asset prices.

An implicit guarantee exists if — as a result of public political pressure — the government is obliged to bail out non-performing private, community-based or social security schemes (as, for example, *Baô-Kur,* the public system for the self-employed in Turkey). Even if governments resist pressure to bail out schemes in serious financial trouble, they may well end up paying far more in social assistance benefits to the people whose other benefits (i.e. pensions or short-term cash benefits) go unpaid or have to be reduced.

---

[5] In this connection it may be noted that under Convention No. 102 any ratifying State shall accept general responsibility for the due provision of benefits; it shall ensure in particular that the necessary actuarial studies concerning financial equilibrium are made periodically and, in any case, prior to any change in benefits, the rate of insurance contributions, or the taxes allocated to covering the contingencies in question.

Thus, through explicit or implicit financial guarantees, governments provide reinsurance for public and private social transfer systems, even if they do not directly finance benefits. Governments remain the ultimate guarantor of national social security schemes and have to exercise their supervisory function accordingly.

Globalization and social security financing

While for a long time the choice of the actual national mix of social protection and public finance instruments was a matter of national preferences and consensus, today global pressures leave their mark on many national policy choices. For the time being such pressures can only be relieved — albeit imperfectly — by domestic policy measures. Governments may not have exhausted all domestic policy means to increase revenues and contain costs without an outright reduction of protection levels. Financing could be switched to general income taxation and specific consumption taxes. In addition measures to reduce dependency could be introduced, for example by raising the retirement age. Simultaneously production processes have to be adapted to accommodate an older workforce.

And yet it is not difficult to foresee that the increasing interconnectedness of world markets may further modify the architecture of social protection financing. Financial globalization has proceeded apace in recent years, at the same time as the role of financial markets in the financing of pension schemes has increased. Major second-tier pension schemes and in future the reserve funds of public pension schemes (for example those in Canada, France and Ireland) will be or are already leading players on the international financial markets. As the performance of these markets is interconnected, pension entitlements of many workers around the world are already highly interdependent. If one major stock exchange crashes, or if stock markets collectively mark down asset prices, millions of workers around the world are simultaneously affected. Conversely, many jobs depend, directly or indirectly, on the investment decisions of the pension schemes of the industrialized world. The international financial institutions are increasingly lending money for the inception or reform of social security systems. International loan and grant moneys go into national and regional social funds. International aid is providing disaster relief and subsidies to national health systems, etc. In their Heavily Indebted Poor Countries (HIPC) debt initiative the IMF and the World Bank are now tying debt relief to the development of sound national anti-poverty policies. All these developments and initiatives are so far proceeding in an uncoordinated manner.

According to recent ILO estimates it would take only a small fraction of the world GDP to lift most people out of most severe poverty in the poorest countries. Organizing or canalizing transfers and delivering benefits still constitute an enormous challenge for global and national governance. With their debt relief campaign the international financial institutions have made a first step. In 2000 the "Social Summit+5" Special Session of the United Nations General Assembly encouraged interested governments to consider the establishment of a World Solidarity Fund to be financed on a voluntary basis in order to contribute to the eradication of poverty and promote social development in the poorest regions of the world.

It must nevertheless be stressed that the extension of social security remains fundamentally the responsibility of each nation. While the international community may provide crisis-related social assistance (and of course development assistance) the continuing effort required to provide social protection must rest with individual countries.

Conclusions

Social security expenditure, especially in developing countries, is projected to rise as a proportion of GDP, as systems are extended and schemes mature. In the industrialized countries expenditure may also continue to increase if it is not possible in particular to stabilize old-age dependency ratios by increasing the labour force participation of women, young people and older workers. The real challenge is a labour market challenge. Jobs have to be found for all workers.

Social security is essentially about the pooling of risk and, generally speaking, the larger the risk pool, the more reliable the protection provided. Reliance on schemes covering small groups or on individual savings plans creates great benefit disparities and uncertainties as long as they are not stabilized and subsidized through national (or even international) resources.

The extent to which advance funding is used and necessary to finance the provision of benefits depends primarily upon the nature of the benefits and the characteristics of the scheme. But advance funding alone is unlikely to solve any of the long-term structural financial problems of national social transfer systems. From the financial, fiscal, economic and social points of view, the only reliable long-term appropriate strategy for maintaining acceptable levels of social expenditure is to reduce dependency levels.

Social protection may be provided by social security schemes or by private systems. Governments play an indispensable role as financial underwriters of social security schemes and they often also have liabilities, explicit or implicit, in the case of private benefit provision. There are important links between the different national instruments that may be used to finance social protection. In particular, decisions about the role of private schemes have major financial implications both for the finances of public schemes and indeed for the state budget. Finally, there is no general rule as to what constitutes an acceptable limit to compulsory social security contributions and taxation. National social transfer levels reflect societal values rather than economic limits.

However, the long-term challenge in social protection financing is global as well as national. If global economic players are allowed to undermine seriously the power of the nation State to levy taxes and social security contributions, then social security, which achieved such progress in the twentieth century, will face great uncertainties in the twenty-first. Governments must work together to preserve their sovereignty in these crucial areas.

Chapter VI

Strengthening and expanding social dialogue

People and societies have developed different forms of social protection, depending on their needs and their pattern of social and economic development. Social protection can be provided within family and community networks, as well as by institutions of civil society, by enterprises and the commercial market, and by public institutions. In more recent years, the international community — as was made clear by the World Summit for Social Development (Social Summit) in Copenhagen in 1995 and "Social Summit+5" held in Geneva in 2000 — has become more concerned with global social policies.

Previous chapters have shown that social protection is expanding its scope from the world of formal-sector wage employment to that of self-employment and casual labour in the informal economy. A wider group of social actors may therefore have to be included in the process of social security financing and management. This chapter therefore attempts to review various forms of partnership and social dialogue that can enhance the effectiveness and coverage of social protection for all.

Actors in social protection

The main function of social protection is to provide income security and access to health care and basic social services. There are various actors involved here, such as family and local solidarity networks, institutions of civil society, enterprises and the commercial market, government and social security institutions, as well as the international community. The social partners — employers' and workers' organizations — often play an important role in the development and management both of social security and of occupational or complementary schemes within the formal sector of the economy. Trade unions need to be committed to expanding their activities to include the informal economy. Can informal economy workers join existing unions and, if not, what changes are needed? Are special structures and recruitment strategies required? In order to be relevant to informal economy workers, unions must be able to deliver tangible benefits and increased protection.

Family and local solidarity networks

The role of the family in providing income security is essential, irrespective of a country's level of development. Income-sharing within the nuclear family provides income security both for the young and for those (mainly women) who work at home as unpaid carers. The family also tends to be the major source of care for young children and, though to a lesser extent, for adults with disabilities and elderly persons. The role of the extended family in providing income security for adult members who are elderly, sick or disabled varies considerably: in some countries of Africa and Asia it remains extremely important; elsewhere it has been eroded by recent social and demographic developments. Large families were often the best guarantee of income in old age, and for many people who are still not covered by any kind of social security system this continues to be the case. Of course, even if the family is large and income is shared fairly within it, the family income may simply not suffice. The poorest families are sometimes able to call on mechanisms of financial solidarity operating at the level of the local community.

Institutions of civil society

The institutions of civil society which help to maintain income security through social protection are of many kinds: self-help groups providing assistance in kind or in the form of labour, savings societies, associations, cooperatives, mutual benefit societies, religious bodies, charities, etc. Their role and their aims vary according to the national and local context. They may provide benefits in addition to those offered by public institutions, or they may be designed to afford a modicum of social protection for people who are not covered by any other system. Some of them may not have any legal status, as in the case of self-help groups providing assistance in kind or in the form of labour. In general, however, the activities of these groups are governed by law and monitored by the public authorities.

The range of benefits which these institutions can offer is very wide. Some are devoted to food security, others to health insurance or pension provision, others provide compensation for death or disability. They are generally financed from the beneficiaries' contributions, sometimes with subsidies from elsewhere. Because they are so close to the beneficiaries, they are generally able to offer benefits which correspond to the recipients' main priorities.

Some social insurance systems had their roots in mutual benefit societies which became widely established and were ultimately converted into compulsory social security schemes. In certain countries they have continued to play an important role by supplementing the benefits of the compulsory system, for example, in health care or in retirement provision. In other countries their role is limited to certain marginal groups. Overall, their contribution at the global level has increased in recent years owing to spreading marginalization and to the growing gaps in statutory social protection.

Enterprises and the commercial market

Income security can be purchased on the commercial market, for instance, for old age, death and disability. Individual contracts involve high transaction costs and tend not to be very widespread, except in countries where they have been made compulsory or where they benefit from generous tax concessions. They can, however, be important for self-employed persons, for whom alternative opportunities to obtain income security may be quite limited.

Occupational or employer pension schemes are another form of income security provided by the private sector. They may be managed in the case of smaller enterprises by commercial providers, or be self-administered in the case of large companies. The transaction costs of these schemes are much lower than for individual arrangements. Typically, the scheme is not open to people not working in the enterprise concerned, so marketing costs are avoided and collecting the premiums or contributions is straightforward.

While occupational schemes were traditionally established at the initiative of the employer, many are now the subject of collective agreements or indeed in some countries have been made compulsory by law or by decree. Employers' organizations and trade unions have played an important role in the development of occupational pension schemes, not only at the level of the individual enterprise, but also at the industry or sector level. This role may be crucial not just for the negotiation of occupational schemes, but also for their subsequent management. Some industry-wide schemes in such countries as the United States are wholly run by trade unions. As pension funds come to play an ever more important part on financial markets, there is an increasing demand from the primary stakeholders to participate in decisions concerning pension fund investments. With billions of dollars of workers' capital circulating in the global markets, many national labour organizations have taken steps to try to control and redirect these funds in order to advance workers' broader interests.

Government and social security institutions

In most countries the organization and provision of social benefits are mainly the responsibility of the public authorities. In historical terms, the development of national social protection systems often reflected the desire of legislators to harmonize and make compulsory various schemes which had developed in individual companies or sectors. It was a question of gradually ensuring that everyone had access to the same social rights.

The structure of the social security scheme will often determine the arrangements for its administration. Thus, schemes which provide universal and means-tested benefits are more likely to be directly administered by the State. But there is a broad spectrum of institutional arrangements ranging from direct administration by a government department to reliance on private-sector management. Where the social insurance tradition (or the contributory principle) is the strongest, as in France and Germany and throughout most of Africa, Asia and still much of Latin America and the Caribbean, schemes are generally administered by a public institution which is supervised by a board of directors or trustees and which, invariably, is legally autonomous. The board is typically bipartite or tripartite, with representatives of employers, workers and government; sometimes other sections of the community and experts such as bankers or medical professionals may also participate. Day-to-day management of the scheme is in the hands of a chief executive who may be appointed by the board or by the minister.

Particularly in some developing countries, administrative segmentation has been a major cause of the lack of focus and thrust in social protection policies. Government policy-making is often concentrated in the ministry of finance, which tends to have a particular interest in pensions. Various other ministries, such as labour, health, social welfare and civil affairs, may be responsible for different social security schemes, often managed by separate agencies. Depending on the extent of fiscal decentralization, local-level governments may also have some independent role, particularly with regard to social assistance.

The international community

Since the end of the 1980s it has been increasingly acknowledged that the international community should develop its own responsibility for humanitarian and social affairs. Humanitarian actions have been accepted as a first area, because — according to United Nations General Assembly resolution 43/131 of 8 December 1988 — failure to assist the victims of natural disasters and emergency situations "constitutes a threat to human life and an offence to human dignity".

The core labour standards identified by the Social Summit in 1995 as the social floor of the emerging world economy are now the subject of the ILO Declaration on Fundamental Principles and Rights at Work adopted by the International Labour Conference in 1998. The concept of a global social floor can be extended to include the guarantee of basic entitlements with regard to education, health and social protection. With regard to education and health, these entitlements have been formulated as aims by the Social Summit in Copenhagen, i.e. the achievement of universal primary education and an under-five mortality rate below 45 per 1,000 by the year 2015. The follow-up Special Session of the United Nations General Assembly in 2000 recommended the strengthening of "modalities of coverage of social protection systems… to meet the needs of people engaged in flexible forms of employment", but did not formulate quantitative objectives or time frames.[1]

Partnerships for social protection

In addition to strengthening the role of the various actors in social protection listed above, there are a number of ways in which partnerships can be formed among them in order to enhance the effectiveness of social security and extend social protection.

Enhancing the effectiveness of social security

The *State* can shape social security systems and influence their effectiveness in a variety of ways:

● organization and provision of social benefits;

---

[1] United Nations: *Report of the Ad Hoc Committee of the Whole of the twenty-fourth Special Session of the General Assembly*, A/S-24/8/Rev.1 (New York, 2000).

- regulations imposing obligations on employers to provide benefits or obliging commercial insurance companies or private pension funds to maintain prescribed standards;

- fiscal policy, including tax concessions for social security benefits or contributions;

- ratification of ILO social security Conventions and participation in bi- and multilateral social security agreements.

Choices made as to the relative weight given to these different approaches have determined the overall structure of the social security system. This has provided the State with both the responsibility for and the opportunity of determining the extent of its own involvement, the range and level of protection to be provided by the market and by the community, etc., the financial arrangements and the organization and management of schemes.

It has long been considered important that the *social partners,* particularly the representatives of the workers covered, be involved in designing and running social security schemes. The Income Security Recommendation, 1944 (No. 67), states that "the administration of social insurance should be unified or coordinated within a general system of social security services, and contributors should, through their organizations, be represented on the bodies which determine or advise upon administrative policy and propose legislation or frame regulations". Under the terms of the Social Security (Minimum Standards) Convention, 1952 (No. 102), "where the administration is not entrusted to an institution regulated by the public authorities or to a government department responsible to a legislature, representatives of the persons protected shall participate in the management, or be associated therewith in a consultative capacity, under prescribed conditions; national laws or regulations may likewise decide as to the participation of representatives of employers and of the public authorities". Similar requirements are contained in later instruments, such as the Invalidity, Old-Age and Survivors' Benefits Convention, 1967 (No. 128), the Medical Care and Sickness Benefits Convention, 1969 (No. 130), and the Employment Promotion and Protection against Unemployment Convention, 1988 (No. 168).

One reason for the participation of the social partners is the fact that the schemes are, at any rate in the case of social insurance, financed wholly or predominantly by the contributions which employers and workers pay on the basis of labour incomes. However, even in the case of schemes which are financed from general tax revenues and administered by a government department, tripartism can play an important role in improving policies and in making systems more responsive to workers' needs. Other forms of popular participation in these schemes can also serve to enhance them, for example patients' consultative committees in the case of public health services. Convention No. 168 requires that where the administration of employment promotion and protection against unemployment is entrusted to a government department, representatives of the protected persons and of the employers shall be associated in the administration in an advisory capacity.

Within the framework of contributory social security systems, *enterprises* are almost invariably given important responsibilities with respect to the deduction and payment of contributions. In some countries, however, enterprises are obliged under labour legislation to provide certain benefits themselves or to make appropriate arrangements with an insurance company. This technique, known as employer liability, has been widely used in the past for employment injury benefits and maternity benefits. Owing to its numerous shortcomings, it has tended to be replaced by social insurance in these fields. However, in recent years, there has been an important trend towards making the employer liable for the payment of cash sickness benefit or sick pay for the first few days or weeks of absence. (This type of reform has been inspired by research findings which show that short-term sickness absence can be greatly reduced if employers have a financial incentive to take appropriate action to improve the quality of working life and to monitor absence from work.)

In many countries responsibilities for the provision of social protection, especially retirement pensions and health care, are ascribed to enterprises, not explicitly by employer liability legislation, but implicitly by the absence of satisfactory provision through statutory mechanisms. The intentions of the State are usually indicated clearly by the fact that enterprises (and to a lesser extent employees) receive substantial tax concessions if they fulfil these responsibilities. Lower-paid workers in less secure jobs, especially women, tend to benefit less from voluntary employer schemes. Providing social protection in this way rather than through social security can mean much greater inequality in the distribution of benefits.

Legislation or government decisions have in certain countries extended private or occupational pension schemes to cover all enterprises and workers in an industry or even entire sectors of the economy. The resulting system falls somewhere between compulsory social insurance schemes and voluntary private schemes. It combines the advantages of broad coverage and pooling of risk with autonomy from any direct involvement of the State. The sound financial base of such schemes and the absolute requirement for them to be jointly managed by employer and worker representatives create favourable conditions for their functioning. Experience in countries such as Finland, France and the Netherlands suggests that these basic safeguards greatly facilitate the regulatory function of the State. By contrast, in countries which rely widely on individual company schemes, vast regulatory systems have developed, accompanied in some cases by the establishment of pension guarantee mechanisms. The regulations tend to be experienced as burdensome by employers and are difficult to police.

Some countries, particularly in Latin America, have indicated a number of reasons for the privatization of their pension systems. To what extent is privatization the answer for improved governance in social security? The debate is essentially on two levels: one relates to the responsibility for providing it, and thus to its structure, and the other to its management.

At the structural level, those who argue against the principles of social insurance maintain that it over-protects individuals and removes their freedom of choice. It is argued that the State should withdraw to a position in which it provides a minimum level of social protection and then creates and encourages an environment under which private arrangements can be made.

At the administrative or institutional level, it is argued that the social insurance institutions are not subject to market competition (they are effectively monopolies) and they are not required to make a profit. Administrators, according to this view, consequently pay insufficient regard to the financial implications of the decisions they are obliged to make. There has been a tendency to assume that the competitive forces of the marketplace would have a generally beneficial effect. However, experience has shown that it is much more costly to administer individual savings accounts than social security records, that pension fund management companies (for example the *Administradoras de Fondos de Pensiones* (AFP) in various countries of Latin America) have high marketing costs, that levels of concentration among pension funds are high, and that private management companies cannot be relied upon to enforce compliance.

On the other hand, many schemes have recognized the need for improved governance and have either reformed their institutional arrangement to achieve a greater level of real autonomy or involved the private sector in various aspects of their administration. The trend is therefore for public schemes to contract out some of their functions and for other private-sector management concepts and practices to be introduced to improve efficiency and accountability.

Towards social protection for all

The appropriate paths for extending coverage depend on a number of factors, such as the country's level of economic development, the state of the social security system and the degree of informalization of employment. Certain industrialized countries have reached full personal coverage for some contingencies, but not for others. As a result, in these countries extension can be achieved within the context of existing systems. For middle-income developing countries it may be possible, for some contingencies, to achieve universal coverage through existing systems. In other cases, it may be necessary to first develop and support schemes specifically designed to meet the needs of workers in the informal economy. Given the small size of the formal sector in low-income developing countries, it is imperative to give priority to schemes specially designed to meet the needs of informal economy workers.

Microinsurance schemes and areabased schemes

As noted in Chapter III, access to health care is one of the top priorities for workers in the informal economy, especially in low-income countries. The extent to which microinsurance schemes have been successful has depended on the characteristics of the bodies that set up the schemes, on their design and on the context in which they operate. The organization should be based on trust among its members, which is enhanced by factors such as strong and stable leadership, its economic base, the existence of participative structures and a reliable financial and administrative structure. Scheme design should include measures to control fraud and abuse, to promote some form of mandatory participation, to contain costs and to foster preventive and promotive health services. Important context variables concern the availability of good-quality and affordable health-care services (public or private) and a favourable climate for the development of microinsurance schemes.

As noted in Chapter III, most of these schemes remain fairly small, and it is therefore important to know with what mechanisms and under what forms of partnership their coverage can be expanded. One option is for such schemes to form organizations among themselves, which will enable them to achieve various objectives, such as a stronger negotiating power in relation to the government as well as (public and private) health providers, sharing of knowledge and greater financial stabilization through reinsurance. A second approach is to devote more effort to the marketing of microinsurance, as a large percentage of the target population is still not well informed of the benefits of being insured. Linked to this is the need to strengthen the credibility of microinsurance. Subsidization of microinsurance is undoubtedly a promising way to expand its coverage, but this is entirely dependent on the capacity and will of the State to redistribute income through the tax system from the rich to the poor.

However, with the growth of microinsurance schemes, other forms of partnerships may also be necessary. Such schemes may team up with, and/or receive support from, larger organizations in civil society (cooperatives and trade unions for instance). They may also seek to involve private companies and social security agencies that already have a well-functioning administration. Experience with successful scaling-up efforts shows that two sorts of changes are needed: in the culture and organization of participating organizations as well as in linkages and forms of collaboration between organizations.

The role of the government is critical for the successful upscaling of these schemes. Local governments can play an important role in setting up area-based social protection schemes — in partnership with local groups of civil society. At the national level, governments are in the best position to ensure that particular experiences can be replicated to embrace other occupations, sectors and areas. Moreover, governments can create an enabling environment for the development of microinsurance schemes. By means of regulation, they need to clarify the relationship between the role of microinsurance and that of the compulsory social insurance system, in order to prevent contribution evasion and to promote, in the longer term, closer links between the two. In the case of health insurance various functions can be distinguished:

(i) promoting health insurance through recommendations on design (benefits package, affiliation and administration) and the setting-up of a management information system;

(ii) monitoring and regulating microinsurance, possibly within the context of legislation on the efficient and transparent administration of schemes;

(iii) improving and decentralizing the public provision of health care, which is an essential prerequisite for the development of microinsurance in many countries;

(iv) undertaking and organizing training, based inter alia on the promotion and monitoring activities mentioned under (i) and (ii); and

(v) (co-)financing the access of low-income groups to health insurance, possibly through subsidies or matching contributions.

Trade unions and employers could also play a major role in setting up new special funds at the state or provincial levels — for example for construction workers — and in experimenting with area-based social protection schemes. The trade unions would ensure that the benefits provided correspond to the priorities of workers, while employers' organizations could convince their members to comply with their contribution obligations.

Social insurance

As noted in Chapter III, there are various ways in which social insurance programmes can be modified and reformed so as to achieve greater coverage. As the guarantor of such programmes, the government obviously plays a critical role here. However, the social partners can also help achieve the extension of social insurance benefits to regular workers not covered so far, as well as to casual and contract labour employed in formal-sector enterprises. The social partners, and in particular the trade unions, could press for measures to extend effective coverage to workers in small enterprises. Training and awareness-raising, followed by consultation and dialogue with the government, would be the ideal road to greater coverage.

Tax-based social benefits

It is generally better for social assistance and universal benefits to be mainly financed by the central government, since the much greater needs of depressed regions and localities cannot be adequately met otherwise. This guarantees that people in all regions of the country have access to the same basic benefits, which need to be adjusted where necessary for cost-of-living differences. Local and regional governments can add benefits to this basic benefit, for example for housing, food or work. Moreover, local government — in collaboration with local institutions — can play an important role in the effective delivery of benefits.

As noted in Chapter I, demand for temporary social assistance measures — often financed by international sources — has increased in countries affected by wars, disasters and crises. In the long run as well, the international community has promised to contribute to the achievement of social objectives such as the reduction of poverty and universal primary education. Within this context, international resources could be used to finance child benefits, which in particular reduce child labour and foster school attendance, as well as basic social assistance benefits, which — in combination with other policies — would make a significant contribution to the reduction of poverty.

Conclusions

This chapter has examined the role of the various actors involved in income security and social protection, ranging from the family and local solidarity networks to the international community. Central government, workers and employers constitute the core partners, but this partnership will have to be expanded to make social security more effective and to promote social protection for low-income workers in self-employment and the informal economy. There is a need for improved linkages both between central and local governments, and between different ministries (social security, labour, health, finance, etc.). An important role will have to be played by local government, by associations that directly represent workers in the informal economy (such as cooperatives, mutual benefit societies and communities) and by intermediary organizations that work on behalf of low-income (wage) workers. In addition, there may be room for partnerships with private financial institutions, for example in the case of social insurance schemes requiring investment management services or of microinsurance schemes needing reinsurance or other specialized services. At the international level, new roles may have to be assumed by the international community, for example regarding the definition of global social policies and the (co-)financing of some basic social benefits.

Chapter VII

Implications for future ILO work

The previous chapters have reviewed a number of key issues, some of which represent challenges to the application of the concept of social security while others focus attention on weaknesses that limit its effectiveness. At a time when, in many countries, social protection needs have intensified, the mechanisms for addressing them are seen by many as having fallen short of meeting their objectives. And, particularly in developing countries, many of those engaged in some form of gainful employment are denied access even to basic social protection and live on a day-to-day basis on the edge of destitution. However, it is important to put this in perspective and to note, amidst the discussion of problems, the success that many schemes have enjoyed in all regions in providing income security and access to health care for millions of people. The appropriate response to the challenge is thus to focus on remedying these weaknesses and to distinguish them from the concept of social security, which remains valid and strong. This report provides an agenda for the development of reform initiatives which will concentrate on these issues.

The ILO has defined its primary goal as the promotion of opportunities for women and men to obtain decent and productive work in conditions of freedom, equity, security and human dignity. Social security is a key ingredient of the goal of decent work and is recognized as a human right. One of the four strategic objectives of the ILO — to enhance the coverage and effectiveness of social protection for all — is directed at giving effect to this right. The mandate and structure of the ILO are uniquely relevant to this challenge as they — and indeed the goal of decent work — both point to the need for linkages between employment and social protection policies. The implications for the ILO programme and its envisaged structure are discussed in this final chapter.

In order to address this objective, the ILO is developing an integrated programme with the following core components:

- research and policy development;
- providing a normative framework through standard setting; and
- technical cooperation and other means of action.

Research and policy development

The objective here is to strengthen the ILO's knowledge base on the extension of social protection, and on making schemes more effective and more equitable. This calls for research and analysis of problems in providing effective coverage, in the financing of schemes and in their governance, and a comparison with other schemes where reform initiatives have been successful. The aim is: (i) to better understand the nature, cause and effect of weaknesses in schemes; (ii) to formulate strategies for the development of effective social protection mechanisms; and (iii) to develop an ILO social protection policy framework through the following components.

(i) *Analysing weaknesses in coverage and effectiveness by:*
- reviewing statistical trends on coverage and social expenditure to document the extent of exclusion;
- collecting data on the employment, income and expenditure situation of non-covered groups, including those in the informal economy, to examine the need for social protection and contributory capacity at the household and local levels;
- identifying the factors contributing to exclusion from coverage;
- identifying the factors which limit the effectiveness of schemes.

The Social Protection Sector is responsible for a special programme on the extension of coverage. In the present biennium this will include research on the statistical trends on coverage and social expenditure as well as on the effectiveness of efforts to extend social protection. Consideration could be given to establishing a social protection observatory to monitor progress in the operationalization of the decent work concept.

(ii) *Identifying and developing effective social protection mechanisms by:*
- assessing the effectiveness of efforts to extend social protection through statutory social security and microinsurance schemes and the linkages between them;
- reviewing the role of the social actors to identify the conditions under which they can work together to extend or improve social protection;
- testing options for design and financing by exploring the feasibility of schemes:
  — for special sections of the labour force;
  — financed from tax revenue rather than contributions;
  — for supporting micro-insurance schemes through mechanisms such as reinsurance;
  — for international financial support for basic social protection in the least developed countries;
- exploring various options for emergency benefits to meet social protection needs in countries affected by a crisis or natural disaster and for the subsequent (re)construction of social security systems;
- establishing linkages between social protection and employment policies, for example between microinsurance and micro-enterprise development programmes and between unemployment benefit schemes, social assistance and active labour market policies;

- identifying ways for social protection to contribute to gender equality through the design of benefits that guarantee equality of treatment and reduce inequities both in the labour market and in the division of work between men and women.

(iii) *Developing an ILO policy framework* to take account of research and experience which provide the basis for policy guidance on enhancing the coverage and effectiveness of social protection schemes. This may, inter alia, imply the evolution of new or alternative national or international strategies to finance social transfer systems.

It should be recalled that the relevant ILO standard-setting activities flow in part from the research conducted into the development of social security. Such research would seek notably to determine any gaps in the areas of social security covered by "up-to-date" standards and to evaluate the overall real impact of these standards among member States.

Providing a normative framework through standard setting

In principle, everyone has the right to be covered by a social security scheme, and international standards should reflect this right and facilitate its exercise. As noted earlier, however, most ILO social security standards focus on wage earners in the formal sector and do not readily fit the needs and circumstances of the self-employed and those who work on an irregular or flexible basis outside a conventional employer/employee relationship. How should ILO standards contribute to the extension of coverage to those presently excluded?

This is a difficult area, where conflicting considerations are compounded by the complexity and variety of working relationships and by the desire of many employers and even workers to avoid paying contributions. As many workers as possible should be brought within the scope of social security schemes based on the solidarity principles of compulsory membership and uniform treatment. Essentially, persons who have the characteristics of employees, even if temporary or part time, should be treated as employees for social security purposes and their employer expected to comply with the appropriate obligations.

However, all this is easier said than done and the less workers look like "employees" the more difficult the process becomes. For the self-employed or for those in situations where any employer/employee relationship is extremely tenuous, a different approach might be justified. The established self-employed with a place of business or profession could gradually be brought within the scope of the same social security scheme as employees or perhaps covered by a separate scheme based on similar principles. Those working on their own account at a lower level are perhaps best covered by special arrangements, which will vary depending on fiscal and economic factors and on their capacity to contribute, but which would constitute a more basic level of social protection. Consideration may therefore be given to the formulation of standards to promote the extension of social protection on this basis. Such standards could: reaffirm the right to social security as included in the International Covenant on Economic, Social and Cultural Rights; seek commitment from governments and their social partners to elaborate and carry out strategies for extending basic social protection; and adopt statistical indicators for measuring progress towards universal coverage. In addition, standards could provide recommendations on guidelines to design, manage and administer social protection schemes and to develop national and international policies and strategies.

Different levels of social security for different categories of workers are a delicate subject, both in principle and in terms of governance. It is vital to delineate the categories as clearly as possible, since otherwise employers and/or workers will be able to choose which scheme to join and what rate of contributions to pay. That would undermine solidarity and could lead to a widespread downgrading of protection among those already covered.

In addition, new standard setting could be considered in the area of equality of treatment between men and women. As noted in Chapter IV, women are heavily represented in the part-time, low-income, intermittent and precarious jobs, which often fall outside the coverage of social security. Most women also often assume the greater share of parental responsibility and therefore have less time to build up their social security entitlements. Moreover, in most societies, women still have a lower retirement age which, if mandatory, can make it difficult for them to fulfil the qualifying conditions for (full) benefits. Men, on the other hand, also face inequality of treatment, as in many countries survivors' benefits are granted only to widows. New standard setting might therefore embrace: equality of treatment as regards entitlement to old-age benefits; equality of treatment as regards survivors' benefits; the division of pension rights in the event of divorce; and the calculation of, or access to, benefits for parents with family responsibilities.

Of all the branches of social security covered by Convention No. 102, the only one which is not the subject of a special ILO standard is child and family benefits. As an effective means to combat child labour and poverty and to promote gender equality, this might well be considered for future standard setting.

Social and demographic changes since the adoption of Convention No. 102 in 1952 have led to the emergence of new types of social security provision, in particular:

- parental benefits, serving to replace the earnings of parents taking time off work to care for a young or sick child, a subject briefly mentioned in Paragraph 10(3) of the Maternity Protection Recommendation, 2000 (No. 191);

- long-term care insurance, protecting people against the very high costs which they may incur if they become unable to look after themselves and to cope with the tasks of everyday living.

These might also be the subject of new standard setting.

In considering these and possibly other topics, it should be borne in mind that new standard setting may take a number of different forms: new standards; revised standards; or protocols added to existing Conventions. It should be noted that the Governing Body of the International Labour Office has decided that seven social security Conventions are in formal terms "up to date" and has asked member States to inform the Office of the obstacles and difficulties encountered which might prevent or delay ratification and, in some cases, of the possible need to revise the Conventions. To these seven Conventions must be added the Maternity Protection Convention, 2000 (No. 183).

In view of the growing complexity of the factors involved in the development of social security schemes to achieve the objective mentioned at the beginning of this chapter, as well as the interdependence between these factors, it would not be appropriate to engage in any of these various forms of normative action on a piecemeal basis and without a clear idea of the general direction of such action. Although the discussion of the present report will undoubtedly provide useful insights in this respect, the complexities and technicalities involved in the subject justify a much more specific exercise. Social security standards would appear in that respect to be a good candidate for the application of the new "integrated approach" for future normative action which the Governing Body approved on a trial basis at its 279th Session in November 2000.[1] The first stage of this approach is to make an inventory of existing standards and standards-related activities in the area chosen. This in-depth analysis is then to be examined in a tripartite discussion at the International Labour Conference and would result in the drawing-up of an integrated plan of action in the area considered. Such a plan of action would identify potential new subjects for standard setting, specify the purpose and form of new and revised standards, give directions for the promotion of existing standards and outline areas for relevant technical cooperation. The discussion could also identify questions which, because of their technical nature or other reasons, are not suitable subjects for a Convention or Recommendation and should be dealt with in other forms such as codes of practice or handbooks. In the third phase, the Governing Body would draw relevant conclusions from the Conference discussion in the context of its regular procedures, including the selection of items for standard setting and revision for the agenda of the Conference.

Given the importance of this subject-matter, the present discussion could be considered as an initial exchange on social security issues, challenges and prospects which would allow for a clarification of the ILO's future activities in this area. Against the background of the outcome of this discussion, and should the Conference deem it appropriate, the Office could then initiate an in-depth examination of ILO standards-related activities in the area of social security within the context of the integrated approach.[2] The Governing Body would be able to examine the timing of this process in the light of comments made at the Conference.

Technical cooperation and other means of action

The International Labour Office, whether through its Social Protection Sector, or through social security specialists in multidisciplinary teams, provides technical

---

[1] For full details, see GB.279/4.

[2] It should be recalled that at its 282nd Session (November 2001) the Governing Body will examine the question of follow-up on consultations concerning social security instruments resulting from decisions by the Governing Body based on the recommendations by the Working Party on Policy regarding the Revision of Standards of the Committee on Legal Issues and International Labour Standards. See GB.279/11/2, Appendix I, para. 54.

advisory services and implements technical cooperation programmes which correspond to the requests of member States concerning social security. A key objective in the ILO's social security programme is to strengthen the capacity of governments, social security schemes, social partners and, where appropriate, NGOs to ensure the long-term sustainability of reforms, and training programmes are given high priority in most technical cooperation projects. Social protection policies should be based on sound financial, fiscal and economic analyses, and the ILO will continue to provide actuarial services and social budget analyses to its constituents. In addition, the QUA TRAIN initiative will provide specific university-level training to financial managers in these systems.

More and more countries are asking the ILO for technical assistance on the extension of social protection either to non-covered sections of the labour force or to new or previously unprotected contingencies. There is clearly considerable scope for existing social security schemes to extend coverage to more people and to more contingencies, but often a prerequisite is technical assistance to address governance and legislative weaknesses and to build the capacity which institutions need if they are to assume new responsibilities. This may include an in-depth analysis of the financial structure of the scheme, which may be conducted in a macro context through a social budget analysis.

A second field of action is to assist governments and the social actors with the formulation of a comprehensive social protection policy. In the field of statutory social insurance, the ILO provides extensive technical assistance with policy development, preparation of draft legislation and administrative implementation of health, old-age, disability, death, employment injury, sickness, maternity and family benefit schemes. Highest priority is given to technical assistance concerning the extension of social protection to groups not currently covered. The ILO also assists with the development and administration of social assistance schemes that are affordable for low-income countries and consistent with other anti-poverty policies.

In some countries, the ILO, and its STEP programme in particular, has focused attention on health insurance, which is one of the key unmet social protection needs for workers in the informal economy. The ILO provides assistance with carrying out feasibility studies, with the aim of assessing how and under what conditions these pilot activities could be successfully implemented and replicated. On the basis of experience gained, the ILO is developing practical tools and training materials for the various social actors to help them to formulate their own policies and activities with regard to microinsurance, and it is also providing network services for social and labour groups involved in microinsurance.

The introduction of social security provisions for those not currently covered will probably necessitate the preparation of manuals of practical guidance and the wide distribution of information concerning such provisions. Existing ILO standards should provide the framework for technical cooperation and research should be carried out on the synergies between standards, technical assistance, meetings and activities of the field structure, with a view to ensuring that these activities correspond as closely as possible to the objectives of the Organization.

Suggested points for discussion

1. How does the changing global context affect the ability of member States to maintain or extend social security provision?

2. In most countries, adequate social security continues to be enjoyed by only a minority of the population. Why is this the case? How can ILO member States and the social partners succeed in making the right to social security a reality for all? How can economic constraints and development levels be taken into account in strategies for achieving this goal?

3. What priority should be placed on extending social protection in small workplaces, among the self-employed, among migrants and in the informal economy? What instruments and policies are likely to be most effective for these groups? What role could microinsurance play?

4. How can strong social security systems sustain a flexible and dynamic labour market and increase the productivity of enterprises and economies?

5. What is the best means of providing income security for the unemployed at different levels of development and industrialization? How can this best be combined with measures to support labour market access and return to work?

6. How can social protection policies contribute to the promotion of gender equality? Is it enough to guarantee equal treatment of men and women in social security schemes? What recent reform measures have helped most to promote gender equality?

7. Does social security face an ageing crisis? Can it be avoided by changing the system used to finance pensions? Or is it necessary to stabilize overall dependency rates by increasing labour force participation, notably of older workers and of women?

8. What are the advantages and disadvantages of alternative methods of financing social security, taking into account differences in ability to contribute to social insurance systems? Do employer social security contributions affect labour costs and employment levels? Can private provision ease the financing of social security without undermining solidarity and universality?

9. How can an expanded social dialogue, both within countries and at the international level, contribute to the extension and improvement of social security? What could be the role of workers' organizations and employers' organizations in that context?

10. How can synergy be best promoted between social security and other dimensions of the overall goal of decent work?

11. What should be the long-term priorities for the ILO's research, standard-setting and technical assistance work in the social security field?

12. Taking into account the integrated approach to standard setting approved by the Governing Body in November 2000, how should this new approach be applied in the social security field?

Statistical annex

Public social security expenditure

Country	Total social security expenditure (percentage of GDP)			Pensions (percentage of GDP)			Health care (percentage of GDP)			Total social security expenditure (percentage of total public expenditure)	
	1985	1990	1996	1985	1990	1996	1985	1990	1996	1990	1996
All countries*		14.5			6.6			4.9			
Africa		4.3			1.4			1.7			
Asia		6.4			3.0			2.7			
Europe		24.8			12.1			6.3			
Latin America and											
Caribbean		8.8			2.1			2.8			
North America		16.6			7.1			7.5			
Oceania		16.1			4.9			5.6			
Africa											
Algeria[4]	...	7.6	...	...	3.3	...	...	3.4	...	...	...
Benin	0.7	1.3	2.2	0.5	0.4	0.2	...	0.5	1.7	...	...
Botswana[3,6]	4.0	2.5	2.7	...	...	...	2.9	2.3	2.3	6.9	7.4
Burundi	...	1.8	2.2	0.1	0.2	...	...	0.8	0.8	...	10.0
Cameroon[7]	1.7	2.2	...	0.4	0.2	...	0.7	0.9	1.0	10.7	...
Cape Verde	...	5.0	...	...	0.2	...	...	3.6	...	...	...
Central African Rep.	...	1.9	...	...	0.3	...	...	1.0	...	...	...
Congo[3]	...	2.2	4.2	0.7	0.9	...	...	1.5	3.2	...	...
Egypt[2,7]	4.8	4.8	5.4	2.3	...	...	1.1	0.9	0.9	15.7	15.8
Ethiopia[7]	3.4	3.2	3.7	1.1	1.0	0.9	0.8	0.9	1.0	11.1	14.9
Ghana	...	2.2	3.1	...	0.0	1.1	...	1.3	1.0	...	18.9
Guinea	...	...	...	...	...	...	...	1.2	1.2	...	...
Kenya	...	2.6	2.0	...	0.4	0.3	...	1.7	1.7	...	7.5
Madagascar	2.2	1.6	1.3	0.5	0.2	...	...	1.1	1.1	...	...
Mali	1.6	3.1	...	1.0	0.4	...	...	1.6	1.2	...	...
Mauritania	...	1.0	0.8	...	0.2	0.2	...	...	...	...	...
Mauritius	3.4	4.8	6.0	3.2	3.2	1.8	...	1.9	1.9	21.6	26.5
Morocco[2]	1.7	2.4	3.4	1.6	0.5	...	...	0.9	1.0	8.4	10.1
Mozambique	...	...	4.7	0.1	...	0.0	...	4.4	4.6	...	...
Namibia	...	...	3.9	...	...	...	...	3.3	3.7	...	...
Niger	...	1.9	...	...	0.1	...	...	1.5	...	...	...
Nigeria	...	1.0	...	...	0.0	...	...	1.0	...	...	...
Senegal[4]	...	4.3	...	1.2	1.0	...	...	2.8	2.5	...	...
Seychelles	...	...	11.6	...	...	...	...	3.5	4.1	...	22.4
Togo	1.2	...	2.8	0.9	...	0.6	...	1.3	1.2	...	...
Tunisia	6.0	7.0	7.7	3.6	2.3	...	...	2.1	2.2	20.3	23.6
Zambia	0.8	...	2.5	0.4	...	...	...	...	2.2	...	...

Country	Total social security expenditure (percentage of GDP)			Pensions (percentage of GDP)			Health care (percentage of GDP)			Total social security expenditure (percentage of total public expenditure)	
	1985	1990	1996	1985	1990	1996	1985	1990	1996	1990	1996
Asia											
Azerbaijan	...	9.5	8.4	...	2.7	...	...	2.9	1.6	...	40.8
Bahrain[2]	...	3.4	4.2	0.2	0.6	...	...	2.6	2.9	10.0	13.7
Bangladesh	...	...	...	0.0	0.0	...	...	...	1.2	...	...
China[2]	...	5.2	3.6	...	2.6	1.5	...	1.4	2.1	...	23.9
Cyprus[7]	8.0	8.1	10.3	4.7	4.5	6.4	1.9	1.9	2.0	24.7	30.2
India	...	1.7	2.6	...	...	...	...	0.9	0.9	...	24.7
Indonesia	...	...	1.7	...	...	0.0	...	0.6	0.6	...	9.8
Iran, Islamic Rep. of	...	4.7	6.1	...	0.5	...	...	2.1	2.1	21.5	18.7
Israel	15.2	14.2	24.1	...	5.9	5.9	3.6	2.7	7.6	27.5	47.4
Japan[2]	11.4	11.3	14.1	5.2	5.5	6.8	4.7	4.6	5.6	35.8	37.4
Jordan	...	6.8	8.9	0.3	0.6	0.5	...	1.7	2.9	...	...
Kazakhstan[1]	...	...	13.6	...	...	...	...	...	3.3	...	50.9
Korea, Rep. of	...	4.1	5.6	...	0.9	1.4	...	1.7	2.1	22.3	21.2
Kuwait	...	9.4	9.6	1.5	3.5	...	...	3.5	2.7	20.7	23.2
Malaysia	2.0	2.7	2.9	1.9	1.0	...	...	1.5	1.4	8.9	13.4
Mongolia[3]	...	...	8.8	...	...	...	...	...	4.1	...	26.4
Myanmar	...	...	0.7	0.0	...	...	...	1.1	0.5	...	6.1
Pakistan	1.1	...	...	0.3	...	0.0	0.8	0.8	0.8	...	...
Philippines	...	1.7	...	...	0.5	...	0.8	0.8	1.3	...	...
Singapore	...	...	3.3	...	...	1.4	...	1.8	1.3	...	...
Sri Lanka	2.5	...	4.7	2.4	...	2.4	...	1.6	1.5	...	...
Thailand	...	1.5	1.9	...	...	...	...	1.0	1.3	10.1	11.9
Turkey[2]	3.9	5.9	7.1	1.9	3.3	3.8	1.1	1.0	2.3	...	27.0
Europe											
Albania[2]	...	...	10.9	...	...	5.7	...	...	2.4	...	35.0
Austria[2]	24.4	24.2	26.2	14.0	13.9	14.9	5.1	5.3	5.8	49.1	49.4
Belarus	...	15.1	17.4	...	5.5	8.8	...	2.6	5.0	...	50.0
Belgium[2]	27.5	25.6	27.1	12.3	11.2	12.0	6.0	6.7	6.9	47.4	50.1
Bulgaria	...	16.5	13.2	...	8.7	7.1	...	3.7	3.3	25.3	24.3
Croatia	...	...	22.3	...	...	8.2	...	...	7.2	...	47.8
Czech Republic	...	16.0	18.8	...	7.3	8.1	...	4.6	6.8	...	38.6
Denmark	25.9	28.7	33.0	7.5	8.2	9.6	5.3	5.3	5.2	47.9	52.5
Estonia[5]	...	13.1	17.1	...	5.3	7.6	...	2.8	5.8	40.3	50.6
Finland	23.4	25.2	32.3	10.3	10.6	13.2	5.7	6.5	5.4	53.8	53.8
France[2]	27.0	26.7	30.1	12.0	12.2	13.3	6.5	6.6	8.0	53.4	55.3
Germany	26.3	25.5	29.7	11.1	10.3	12.4	7.2	6.7	8.3	54.3	52.1
Greece[2]	19.5	19.8	22.7	11.6	12.7	11.7	3.3	3.5	4.5	57.8	67.4
Hungary	...	18.4	22.3	...	10.5	9.3	4.1	5.9	5.4	35.4	35.8
Iceland	7.3	15.7	18.6	3.5	2.8	5.7	3.6	7.7	7.5	38.2	47.0
Ireland	22.9	19.2	17.8	6.6	5.9	5.1	6.6	5.9	5.1	47.0	50.2

Country	Total social security expenditure (percentage of GDP)			Pensions (percentage of GDP)			Health care (percentage of GDP)			Total social security expenditure (percentage of total public expenditure)	
	1985	1990	1996	1985	1990	1996	1985	1990	1996	1990	1996
Italy[2]	21.6	23.1	23.7	12.5	13.5	15.0	5.5	6.3	5.4	42.9	45.5
Latvia	...	...	19.2	...	6.1	...	...	...	4.0	...	45.5
Lithuania	...	...	14.7	...	...	7.3	...	...	4.0	...	42.5
Luxembourg[2]	24.0	23.4	25.2	13.0	11.9	12.6	5.5	6.1	6.5	48.4	51.4
Malta	19.0	13.3	20.6	14.4	...	...	3.5	...	4.2	...	48.6
Moldova, Rep. of	...	...	15.5	...	...	7.4	...	...	6.3	...	...
Netherlands	28.9	29.7	26.7	12.2	13.6	11.4	5.9	6.1	6.8	51.6	51.4
Norway[2]	20.0	27.1	28.5	7.3	9.1	8.9	5.7	6.7	7.0	52.7	57.7
Poland	17.0	18.7	25.1	...	8.5	14.3	4.5	5.0	5.2	...	52.1
Portugal	13.2	14.6	19.0	6.4	7.4	9.9	3.9	4.3	5.0	34.9	...
Romania	...	...	12.4	...	...	6.8	...	...	2.9	...	34.7
Russian Federation[2]	...	...	10.4	...	...	...	...	...	2.7	...	26.9
Slovakia	...	15.9	20.9	...	7.8	8.3	...	5.7	6.0	...	...
Spain	18.5	19.6	22.0	9.2	9.4	10.9	4.6	5.4	5.8	45.8	56.7
Sweden	31.1	32.2	34.7	10.1	10.3	13.8	8.1	7.9	6.1	53.0	50.0
Switzerland[2]	17.4	20.1	25.9	9.4	10.1	12.8	4.8	5.3	6.6	44.2	49.3
Ukraine	...	...	19.8	...	...	9.6	...	...	4.1	...	...
United Kingdom[2]	21.1	19.6	22.8	8.3	8.9	10.2	4.9	5.2	5.7	46.4	54.9
Latin America and Caribbean											
Argentina[6]	6.6	9.8	12.4	...	3.6	4.1	1.1	4.4	4.3	35.8	41.2
Bahamas	5.8	4.2	...	1.1	1.0	...	3.3	2.7	2.5	23.7	...
Barbados	...	8.6	10.0	4.0	3.4	4.1	...	3.1	4.4	...	...
Belize	...	3.1	3.5	0.3	0.3	...	...	2.3	2.1	8.7	14.2
Bolivia	...	4.2	7.0	...	2.0	...	...	1.1	2.3	23.8	29.3
Brazil[3]	7.6	10.8	12.2	...	...	2.4	1.6	2.3	2.1	32.0	36.7
Chile	13.5	16.2	11.3	...	6.0	5.9	1.6	2.0	2.3	...	45.6
Colombia[2]	4.8	...	6.1	1.0	0.6	0.9	1.8	...	5.1	...	...
Costa Rica	7.4	10.3	13.0	2.0	...	...	4.1	6.7	6.8	40.1	42.6
Cuba	12.5	15.2	...	6.7	7.0	...	4.8	5.6	...	...	...
Dominica	1.4	2.2	4.8	0.7	0.8	1.4	0.3	0.4	0.4	...	...
Dominican Rep.[6]	2.0	2.1	2.5	...	...	...	1.4	1.6	1.8	18.3	15.7
Ecuador	2.8	2.1	2.0	1.8	1.1	1.2	0.6	0.6	0.3	...	...
El Salvador	1.3	1.9	3.6	0.5	0.7	1.3	0.6	0.8	1.3	...	...
Grenada	...	6.9	...	1.8	2.6	...	...	3.7	2.8	...	...
Guatemala	...	2.4	...	...	0.3	...	...	1.5	1.7	...	...
Guyana	...	4.5	5.8	1.1	0.6	0.9	...	3.4	4.3	...	...
Jamaica	...	4.0	4.5	...	0.6	0.3	...	2.9	2.5	...	...
Mexico	3.4	2.8	3.7	0.3	0.3	0.4	2.9	2.1	2.8	23.7	22.6

Country	Total social security expenditure (percentage of GDP)			Pensions (percentage of GDP)			Health care (percentage of GDP)			Total social security expenditure (percentage of total public expenditure)	
	1985	1990	1996	1985	1990	1996	1985	1990	1996	1990	1996
Nicaragua[3]	...	7.8	9.1	...	...	1.4	...	4.8	4.3	21.6	28.1
Panama	8.0	...	11.3	4.0	...	4.	3.5	...	5.6	...	41.3
Peru	...	...	...	...	...	...	...	1.2	2.2	...	...
Trinidad and Tobago[2]	...	...	6.6	...	...	0.6	...	2.7	2.5	...	22.7
Uruguay	...	14.2	22.4	...	...	8.7	...	1.2	2.0	54.7	67.8
North America											
Canada[2]	16.4	17.6	17.7	4.2	4.8	5.4	6.1	6.7	6.6	36.9	40.1
United States	13.4	14.1	16.5	6.8	6.6	7.2	4.4	5.6	7.6	40.6	48.8
Oceania											
Australia[2]	14.0	14.5	15.7	4.6	4.6	4.6	5.5	5.6	5.7	38.7	41.5
Fiji	...	6.1	...	...	4.0	...	...	2.0	...	...	...
New Zealand	17.6	22.2	19.2	7.9	8.2	6.5	4.4	5.8	5.4	...	...

Notes: Total social security expenditure covers expenditure on pensions, health care, employment injury, sickness, family, housing and social assistance benefits in cash and in kind, including administrative expenditure. Pension expenditure includes expenditure on old-age, disability and survivors' pensions. Health-care expenditure covers expenditure on health-care services.
* Regional averages calculated for listed countries only, using 1996 and 1990 data. Averages weighted by GNP in Purchasing Power Parity dollars.
[1] For 1996: 1997 data.
[2] For 1996: 1995 data.
[3] For 1996: 1994 data.
[4] For 1990: 1989 data.
[5] For 1990: 1991 data.
[6] For 1985: 1987 data.
[7] For 1985: 1986 data.

Sources: Originally published in ILO: *World Labour Report 2000* (Geneva, 2000), statistical annex, table 14. Slightly revised to incorporate new data which arrived after the *World Labour Report* was published. Table includes estimates based on data from ILO Inquiries into the Cost of Social Security, combined with data from the *Government Finance Statistics Yearbooks* 1998 and 1999 (Washington, DC, IMF). For OECD member countries, data from the *OECD Social Expenditure Data Base* (OECD, Paris, 1999) were used when no other source was available or data seemed incomplete. For other countries, where the reply to the ILO Inquiry was not complete, IMF expenditure data on health and social security and welfare were used to estimate total expenditure. GDP data from World Bank: *World Development Indicators 1999* and from the United Nations Statistics Division. Total general government expenditure estimated on the basis of IMF *Government Finance Statistics Yearbooks*.